A-Z DERE

CW01023028

REFERENCE

A Road	**A38**	Car Park (selected)	P
B Road	**B5020**	Church or Chapel	†
Dual Carriageway		Cycleway (selected)	🚲
Tunnel		Fire Station	■
One-way Street		Hospital	H
Traffic flow on A Roads is also indicated by a heavy line on the driver's left.		House Numbers (A & B Roads only)	73 89
Road Under Construction		Information Centre	i
Opening dates are correct at the time of publication.		National Grid Reference	⁴40
Proposed Road		Park and Ride	Meteor Centre P+R
Restricted Access		Police Station	▲
Pedestrianized Road		Post Office	★
Track / Footpath		Toilet	▽
Residential Walkway		Viewpoint	米
Railway	Station / Level Crossing / Tunnel	Educational Establishment	▢
Built-up Area	MILL RD.	Hospital or Healthcare Building	▢
		Industrial Building	▢
Local Authority Boundary		Leisure or Recreational Facility	▢
Post Town Boundary		Place of Interest	▢
Postcode Boundary (within Post Town)		Public Building	▢
Map Continuation	24 / Large Scale City Centre 4	Shopping Centre or Market	▢
		Other Selected Buildings	▢

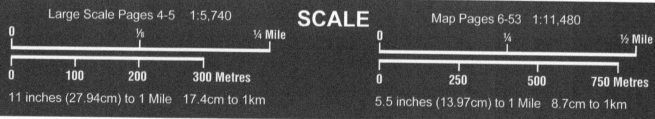

SCALE

Large Scale Pages 4-5   1:5,740

0   ⅛   ¼ Mile
0   100   200   300 Metres
11 inches (27.94cm) to 1 Mile   17.4cm to 1km

Map Pages 6-53   1:11,480

0   ¼   ½ Mile
0   250   500   750 Metres
5.5 inches (13.97cm) to 1 Mile   8.7cm to 1km

EDITION 6   2020

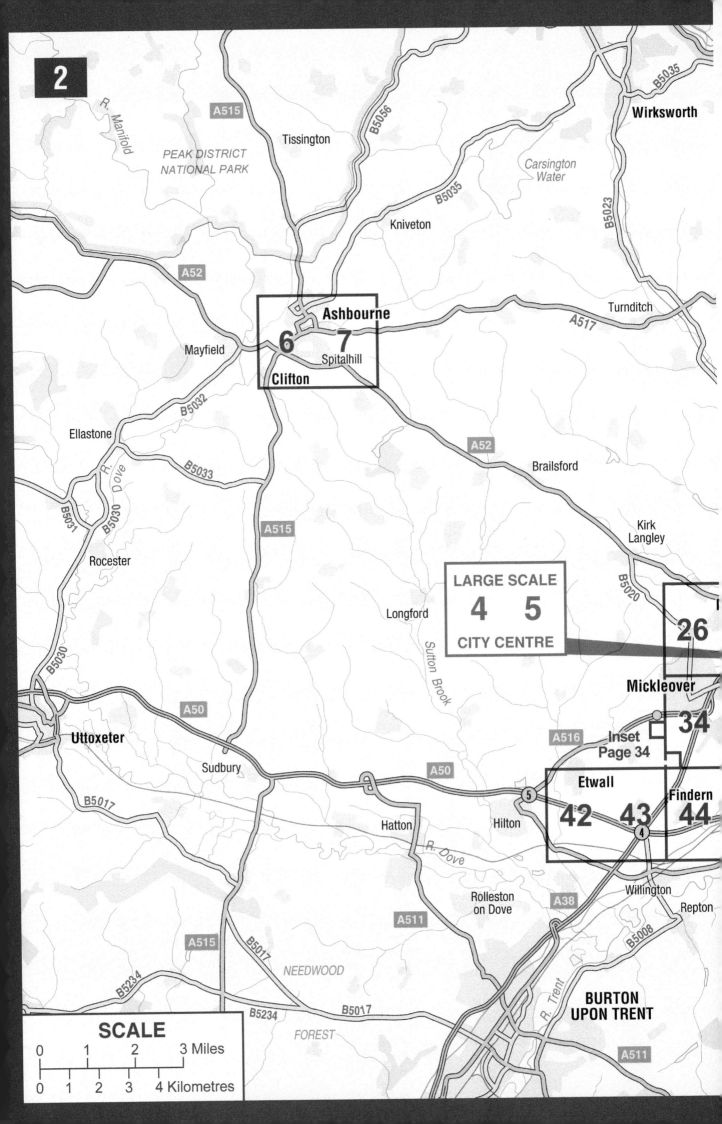

2

R. Manifold

A515

Tissington

B5056

B5035

Wirksworth

PEAK DISTRICT
NATIONAL PARK

Carsington
Water

B5023

Kniveton

A52

Turnditch

A517

Ashbourne

6 **7**

Mayfield

Spitalhill

Clifton

B5032

A52

Brailsford

Ellastone

B5033

R. Dove

B5031

B5030

A515

Kirk
Langley

Rocester

B5020

Longford

LARGE SCALE

4 **5**

CITY CENTRE

26

Sutton Brook

Mickleover

B5030

A50

34

A516

Inset
Page 34

Uttoxeter

Sudbury

A50

Etwall

42 **43**

Findern

44

⑤

B5017

Hatton

Hilton

④

R. Dove

Rolleston
on Dove

A38

Willington

Repton

A511

NEEDWOOD

B5008

B5234

A515

B5017

R. Trent

**BURTON
UPON TRENT**

B5234

B5017

FOREST

A511

SCALE

0   1   2   3 Miles

0 1 2 3   4 Kilometres

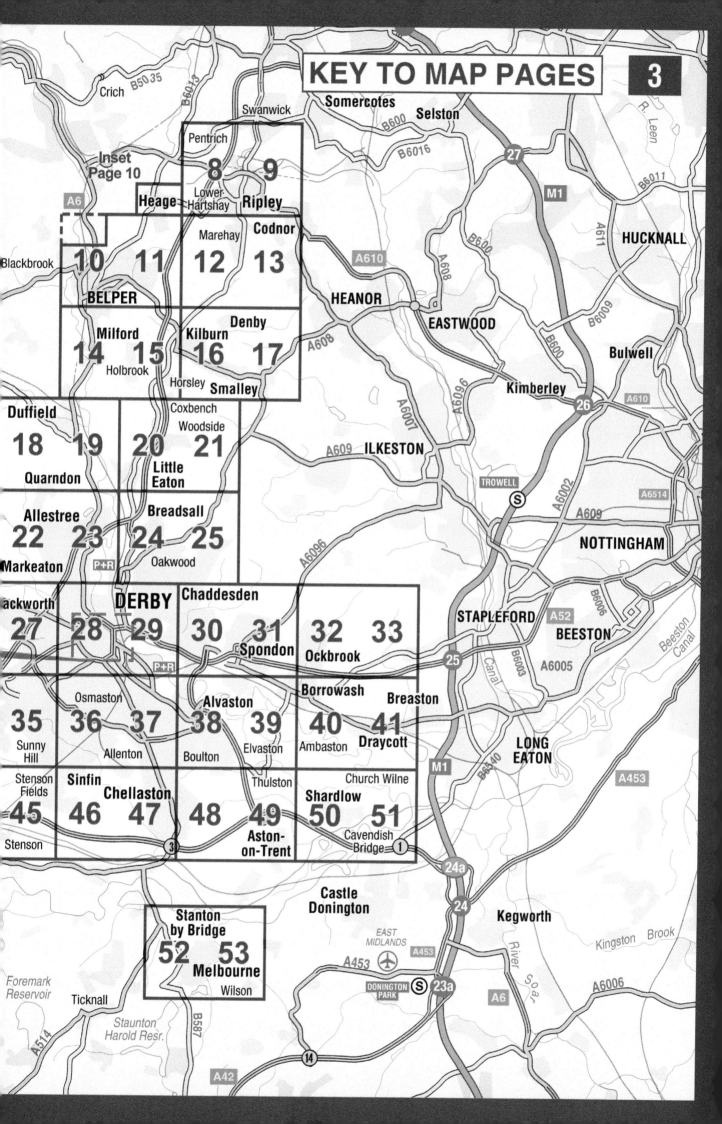

KEY TO MAP PAGES

3

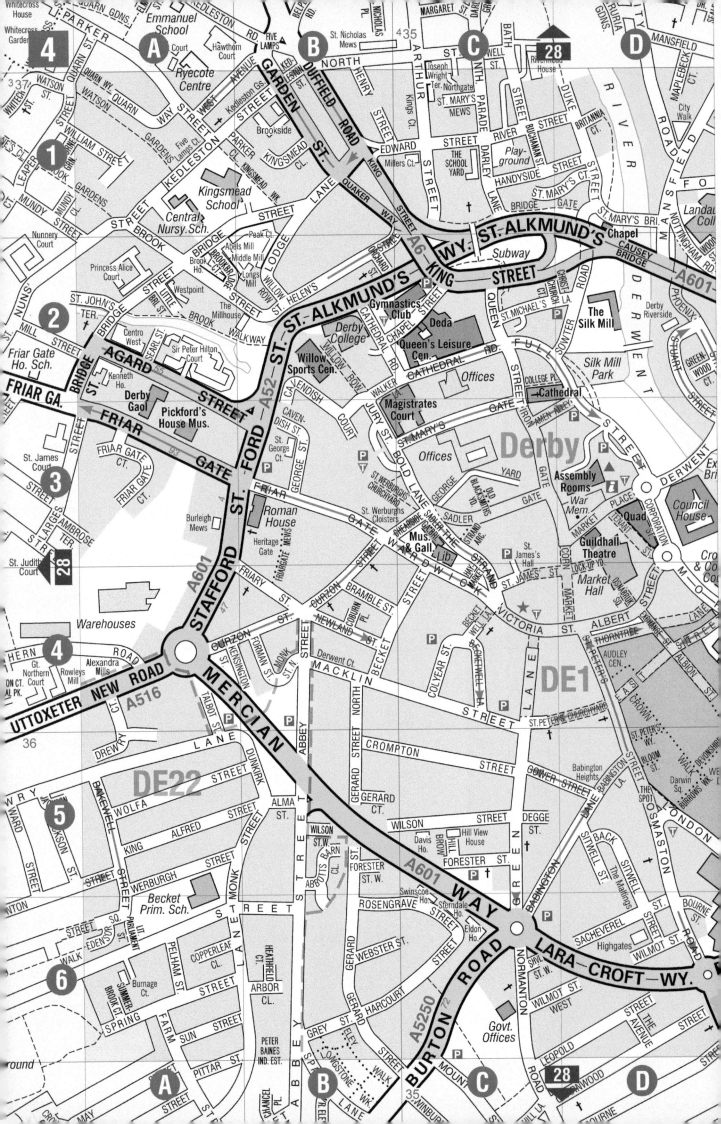

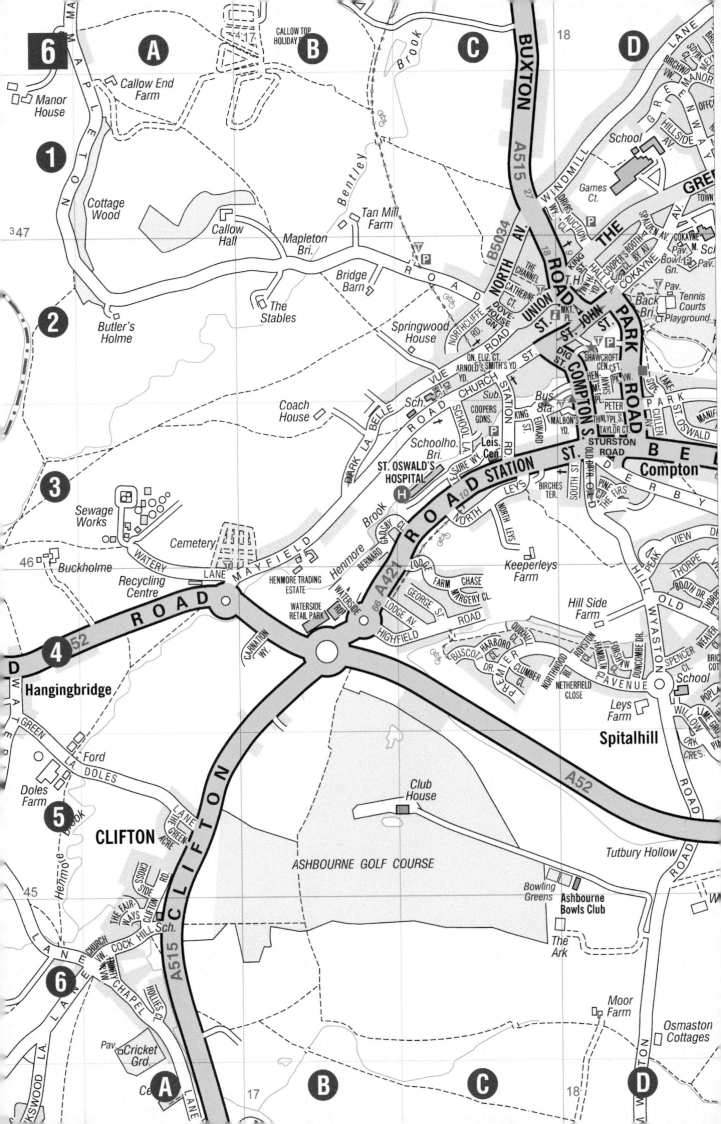

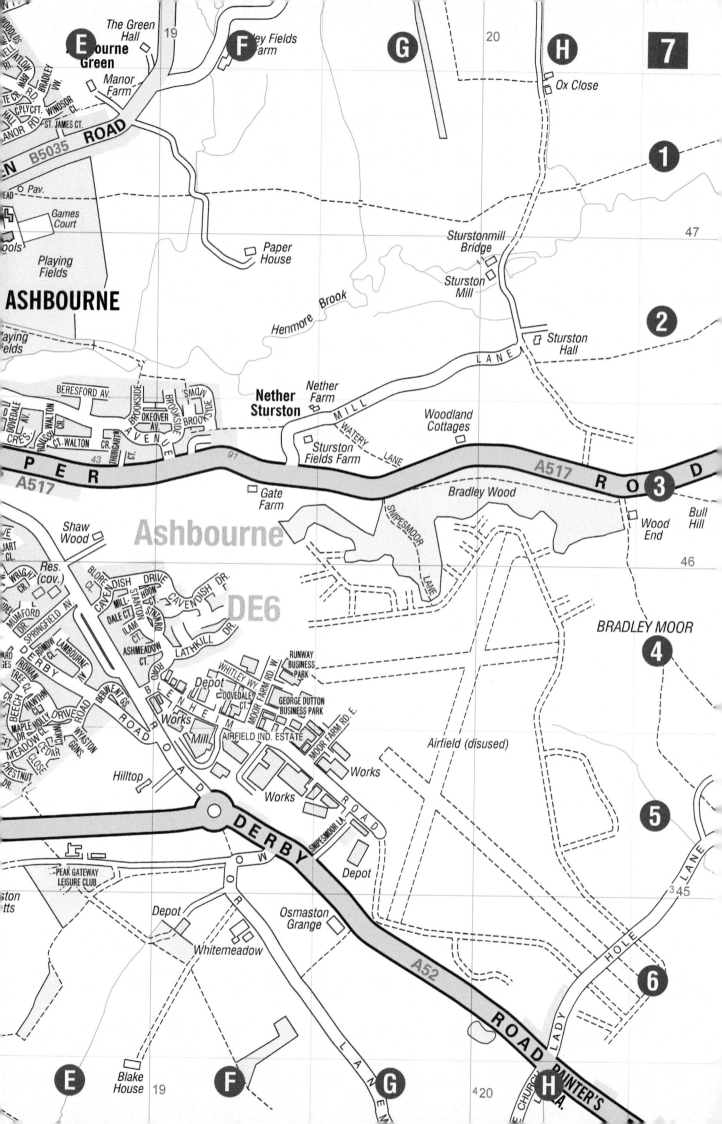

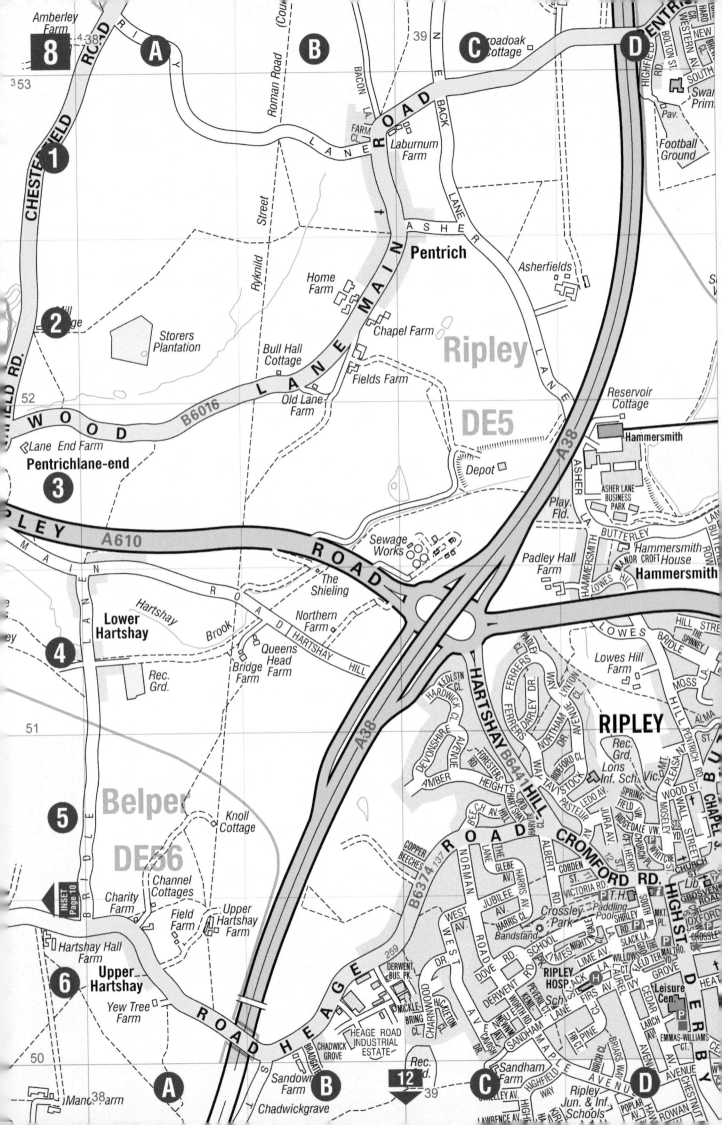

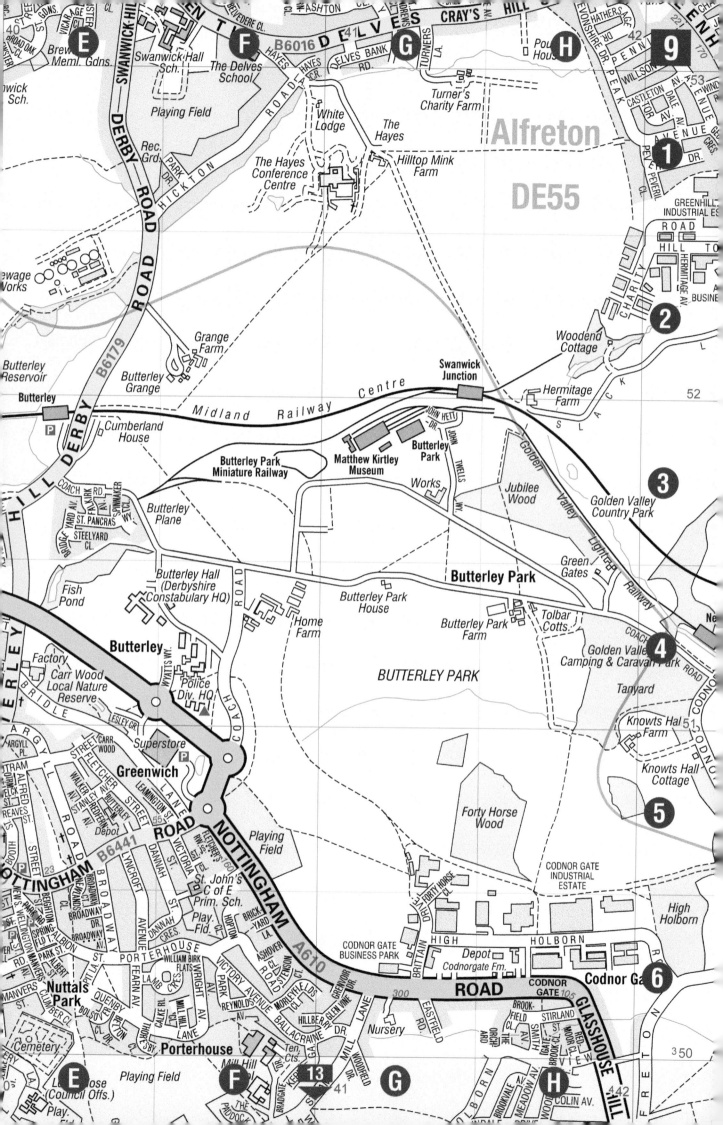

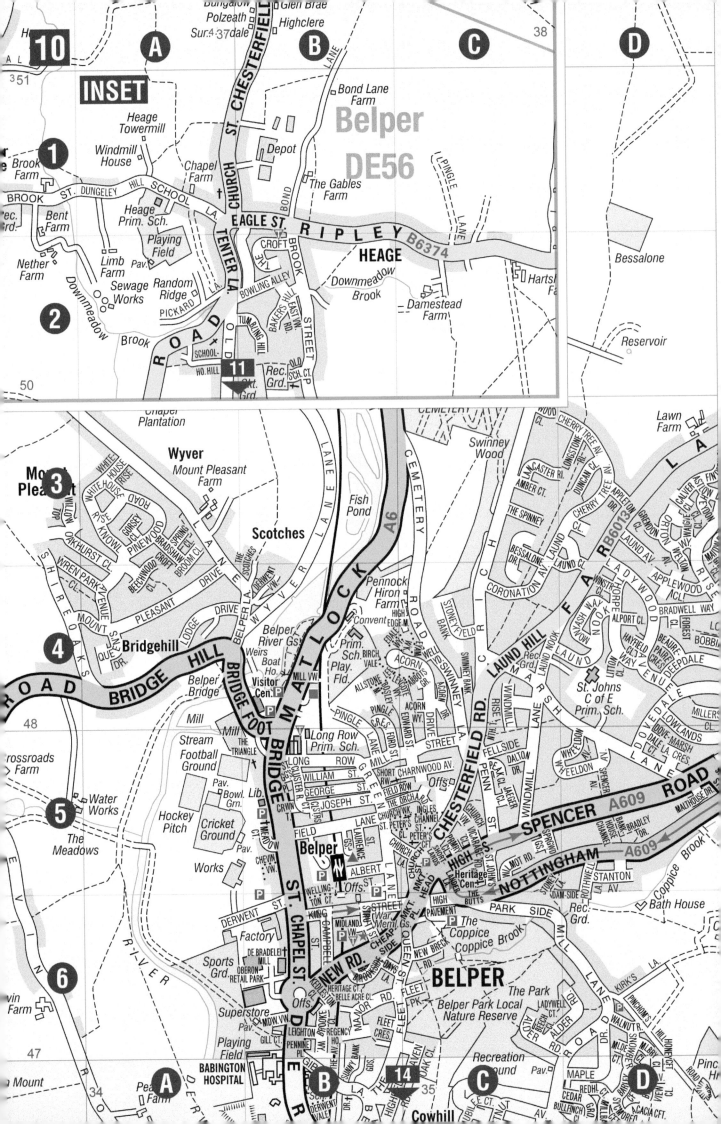

Yew Tree Farm

Manor Farm

Cattle Grid

1

rleypark Farm

West Bank Farm

EDGE DR.
CRICKT VW. DR.
HIGH
MT PLSNT
PENNINE DR.
COOKFIELD
WINDMILL VW.
MEADOW
DOWN

Sycamore Farm

PARK SIDE ROAD

2

Foreclose Farm

The Bent

JACKSON'S

Lodge Farm

NEW LANE

ROAD

PARK CRT.
PARKFIELDS VW.
COTTAGE CL.
PARK ROAD

Parkside Farm

PARK

Morle

Boothgate

Boothgate

BOOTHGATE

Cottage Farm

49

Grangewood Farm

CHESTERFIELD ROAD

UND

Belper DE56

LAUND FM. M.

Far Laund

ASHFORD

MARSTON
NORBURY
EDENSOR
NEWTON CL.
BEELEY CL. DR.
PILSLEY
ARKWRIGHT
WEAVERS CL.
SPINNERS WAY
KINGSWOOD AV.
DENSOR
FALCONS CL.
MERLIN WD.
HARRIER
NAILERS RISE
WAY
PINFOLD
POTTERY CL.
WHITEMOOR HALL
WALCOTE CL.
ASHDONE GS.
WESTRAL
MARLBOROUGH DR.
GREGORYS WY.
CRESCENT
WHITEMOOR WAY

Coppice Brook

Rookery Farm

White Moor

BLENINS
SALISBURY DR.
WARWICK GDNS.
HAREWOOD CL. DR.
SHERBOURNE DR.
MARTIN CLOSE
MORRELL
ROKE KENDRAY DR.
ELSECR SSTON CL.
HOYLAND CT.
SCOTT DR.
CABOT CL.
HILARY CL.
COOK CL.

Morleyhill Farm

Dale Farm

Knob Farm

MORLEY PK.

MORLEY RD.

MORLEY CL.

3

12

Stre

Morrell Close Farm

Morrell Wood Farm

SPINNERS WAY

A38

4

Morrell's Wood

THE HAWTHORNS
HUNTER RD.
ASHOP
NEY WY.
ST. COURT
LEYS CT.
MOULIN CL.
BURBAGE CL.
DRIVE
BRETTON RD.
STOKE CL.
BLACKDEN CL.
ROAD

Playing Field

Playing Field

WICKSTEED CL.

BRAMPTON CT.
JAMES CT.
BEAUMN
WHILTON CT.
CULLWORTH
PYTCHLEY CL.
NASEBY
YARDLEY
OVERSTN WAY

Belper School

Belper Leisure Cen.

Henmoor

ROAD

5

Sch.

ALTON RD.

FARM CL.

JOHN KNOWLE

LECHE CROFT

ASH ACRE

BARTON KNOWLE

WINEGRSS
CLDHAM
JODRELL
ROYAL AV.
GATE
ASHTON W.
BRAFELD CL.
HIGH GRO.
HILLCREST

Whitemoor Cen.

Works

Bullsmoor

KILBOURNE ROAD

Pottery Farm

KILBURN ROAD

Ireton Cottage CT.

IRETON RD.

Park Hall

PARK

KYARD

6

ROAD

 rry House Farm

OPENWOODGATE

BARTON OPENWOOD GATE

LANE

OPENWOOD

Hilltop Farm

3 47

Rec. Grd.

Tooterhill Cottage

Ireton Houses

Sycamore Houses

Rec. Grd.

n's

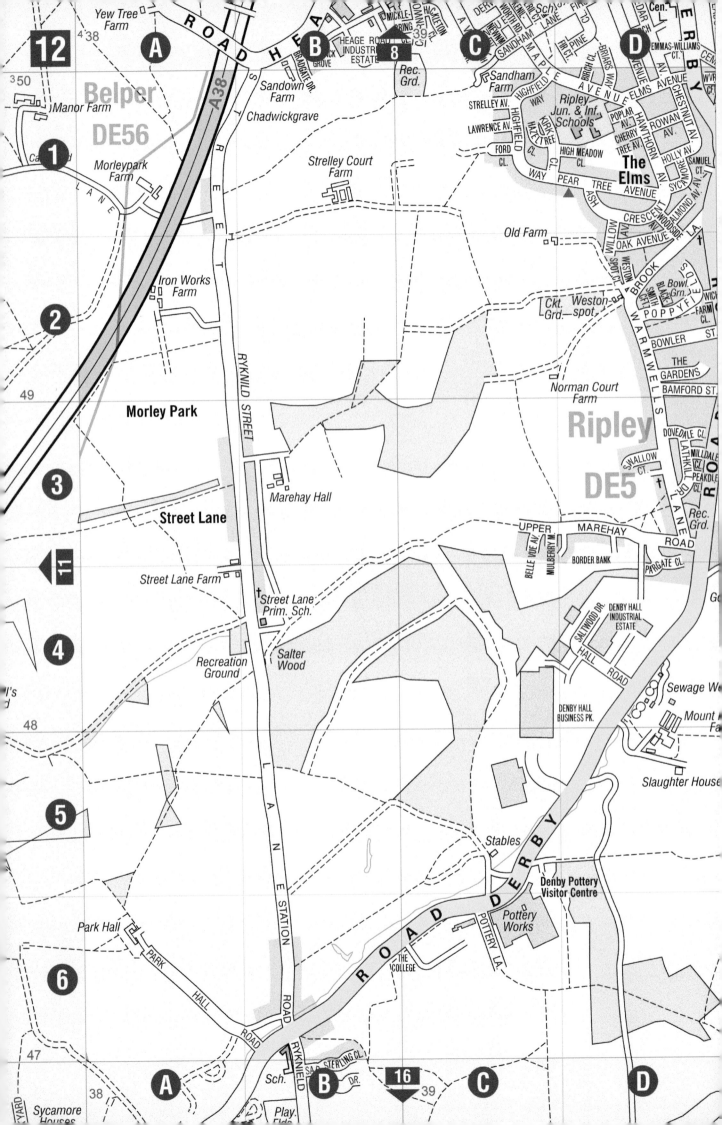

12

Belper
DE56

Ripley
DE5

Morley Park

Street Lane

Yew Tree Farm

Manor Farm

Morleypark Farm

Iron Works Farm

Sandown Farm

Chadwickgrave

Strelley Court Farm

HEAGE ROAD INDUSTRIAL ESTATE

MICKLE-BRING

HICKLETON

Rec. Grd.

Sandham Farm

Ripley Jun. & Inf. Schools

STRELLEY AV.

HIGHFIELD WAY

LAWRENCE AV.

HIGHFIELD CL.

FORD CL.

HIGH MEADOW CL.

The Elms

PEAR TREE

OAK AVENUE

ASH CRESCENT

WILLOW

BROOK

WESTON SPOT CL.

POPLAR AV.

CHERRY TREE AV.

HAWTHORN AV.

ROWAN AV.

HOLLY AV.

SAMUEL CT.

ALMOND AV.

SYCAMORE

Old Farm

Ckt. Grd.

Weston spot.

WARMWELLS LANE

Norman Court Farm

BOWLER

THE GARDENS

BAMFORD ST.

POPPYFI...

SMITH

BLACK...

FARM CL.

DOVEDALE CL.

SWALLOW CT.

MILLDALE CL.

LATHKILL DR.

PEAKDLE CL.

Rec. Grd.

ROAD

RYKNILD STREET

Marehay Hall

Street Lane Farm

Street Lane Prim. Sch.

Salter Wood

Recreation Ground

UPPER

BELLE VUE AV.

MULBERRY M.

MAREHAY

ROAD

BORDER BANK

PARGATE CL.

SALTWOOD DR.

DENBY HALL INDUSTRIAL ESTATE

HALL ROAD

DENBY HALL BUSINESS PK.

Sewage W...

Mount ...

Slaughter House

Park Hall

PARK HALL ROAD

STATION ROAD

RYKNILD

Stables

Denby Pottery Visitor Centre

Pottery Works

POTTERY LA.

DERBY ROAD

THE COLLEGE

Sycamore Houses

EMMAS-WILLIAMS CT.

SAN...STERLING CL.

11
8
16 39

A B C D

1

2

3

4

5

6

A B C D

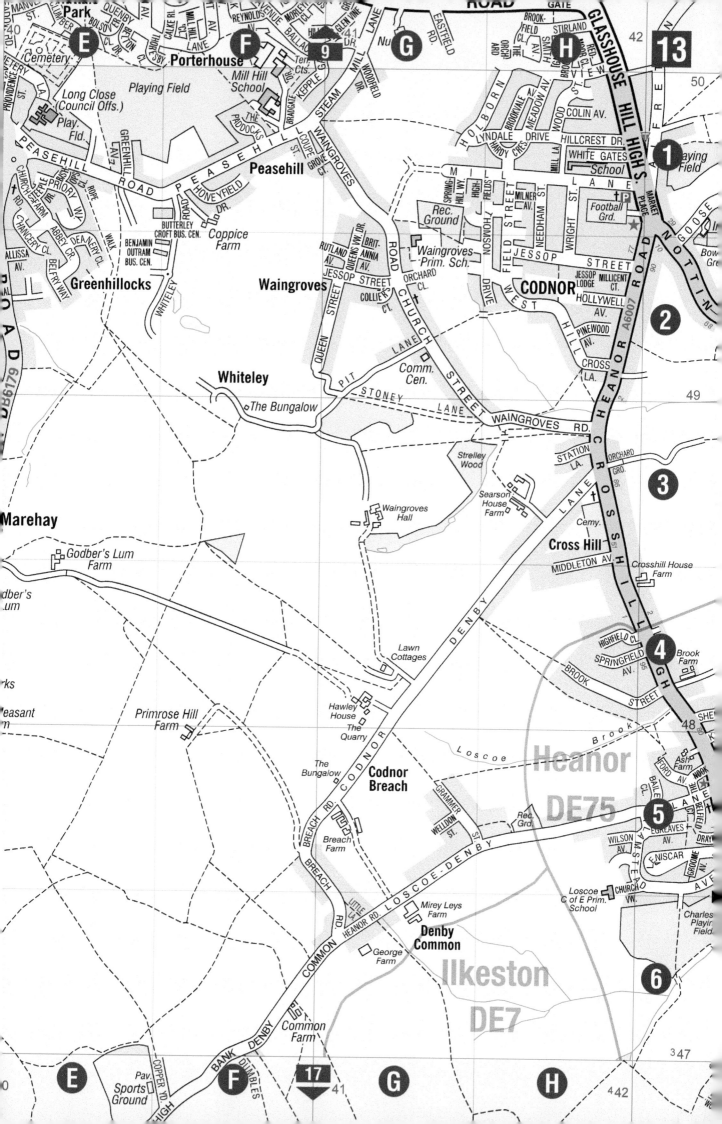

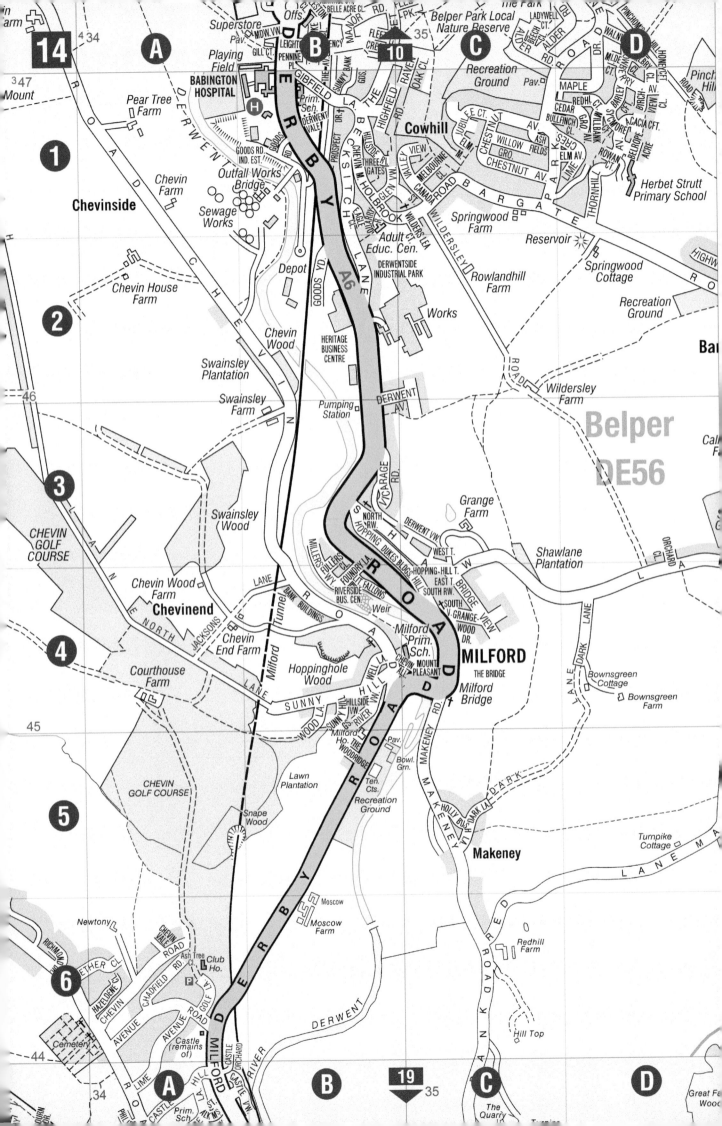

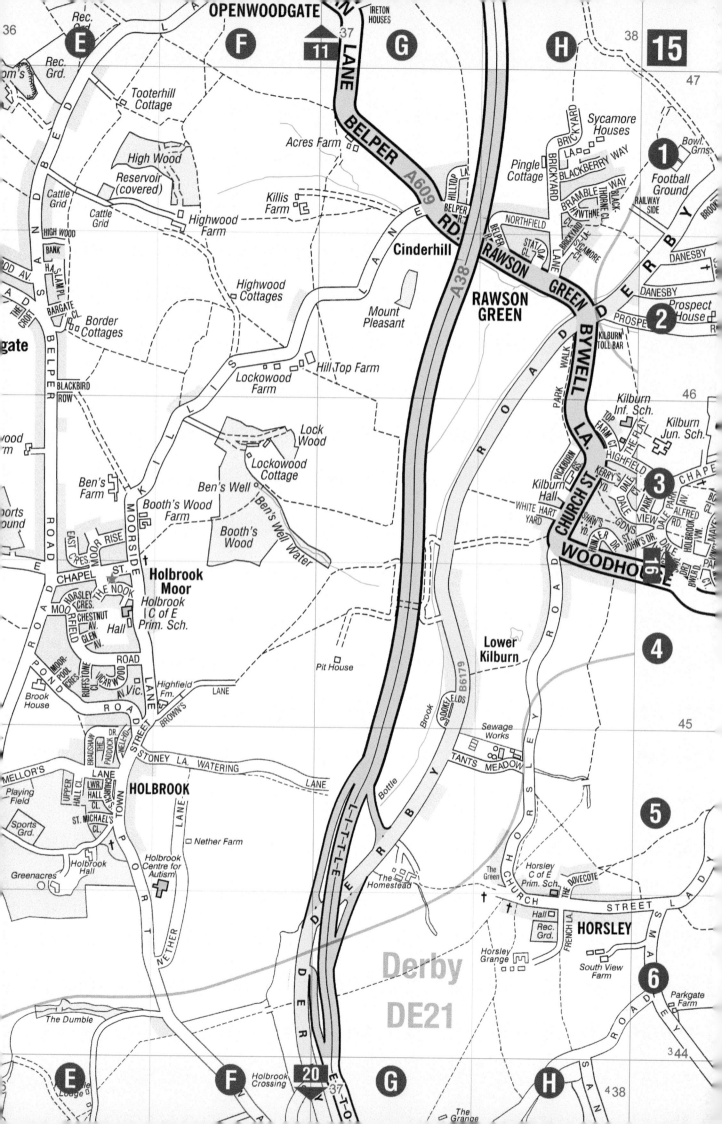

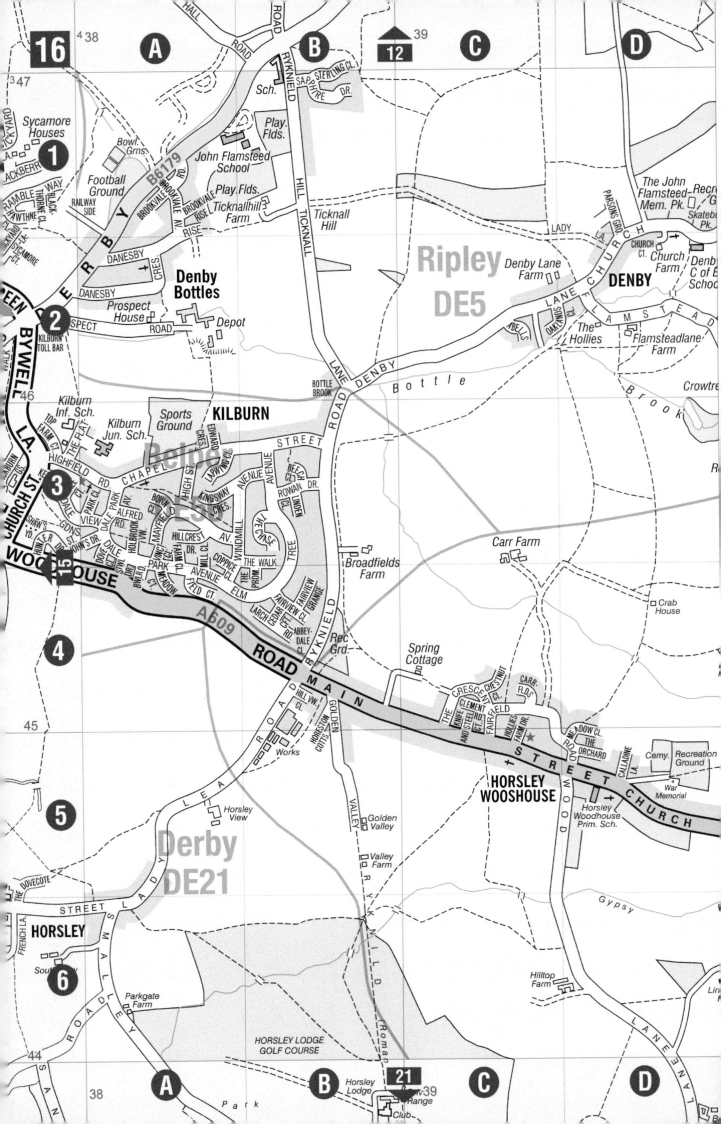

16

A   B   🏠 39   C   D

12

1

3 47

Sycamore
Houses

Bowl.
Grns.

Football
Ground

B6179

John Flamsteed
School

Play. Flds.

Sch.

RYKNIELD

SAPPHIRE
STERLING CL.
DR.

The John
Flamsteed Recr.
Mem. Pk.

Skateb.
Pk.

PARSONS GRO.

RAILWAY
SIDE

BROOKVALE
AV.

Play.Flds.

Ticknallhill
Farm

Ticknall
Hill

HILL
TICKNALL

LADY

CHURCH
CT.

CHURCH

Church
Farm

CHURCH

Denby
C of E
Sch.

DENBY

BRAMBLE WAY
BLACK-
THORNE CL.
HAWTHNE.
SYCAMORE
CT.

DANESBY
CRES.

**Denby
Bottles**

DANESBY

BROOKVALE RD.
BROOKVALE
RISE

RISE

**Ripley
DE5**

Denby Lane
Farm

LANE

FLAMSTEAD LA.

OAK TREE

LANE

ABELLS

The
Hollies

Flamsteadlane
Farm

2

46

KILBURN
TOLL BAR

WALK

BYWELL
LA.

Prospect
House

Depot

Bottle
Brook

LANE

DENBY

ROAD

Bottle

Brook

Crowtre

3

Top
Farm Ct.
THE PLAT

Kilburn
Inf. Sch.

Sports
Ground

KILBURN

STREET

EDWARD
CRES.

Bottle
Brook

ROAD

CHURCH ST.

HIGHFIELD
RD.

Kilburn
Jun. Sch.

CHAPEL

Belper
DE56

BECH
LINDEN
ROWAN
DR.

DALE
KELBURN
GDNS.
PARK CL.
DALE PARK
VIEW
BOWM
DALE
JOHN'S DR.
DOVE
DALE
SHAW'S
YD.
HUNTER DR.

HOLBROOK
WK.
ALFRED
RD.
MAYFIELD
FARM CL.
HILLCREST
DR.
VINCENT
PARK
BWL D.
CT.
MEADOW

HIGH ST.
LAPWING CL.
KINGSWAY
CRES.

AVENUE

AVENUE

AVENUE

THE CHASE

WINDMILL
MILL
FIELD CT.

TREE

LINDEN

Carr Farm

WOODHOUSE

15

COPPICE
CL.
ELM
THE
PROM.
LARCH
CEDAR
CT.
ABBEY-
DALE
CL.

FAIRVIEW CL.
FAIRVIEW
GRANGE

RYKNIELD

Broadfields
Farm

Crab
House

4

A609

ROAD

MAIN

Rec
Grd.

Spring
Cottage

CHESTNUT
CL.
CRESCENT
THE
CLEMENT
KNIFE
AND STEEL
RD.
CT.
FAIRFIELD
CT.

CARR
FLDS.

HOLLIES
FARM DR.

MEADOW CL.
THE
ORCHARD

CALLADINE
LA.

Cemy.

**Recreation
Ground**

War
Memorial

45

ROAD

LEA

HILL VW.
CL.

HORESTON
COTTS.
GOLDEN

Works

VALLEY

Horsley
View

Golden
Valley

**HORSLEY
WOOSHOUSE**

WOOD

Horsley
Woodhouse
Prim. Sch.

STREET

CHURCH

5

Derby
DE21

Valley
Farm

Hilltop
Farm

Lir

6

THE DOVECOTE

STREET

FRENCH LA.

HORSLEY

Southway

LADY

SMALLEY

Parkgate
Farm

RYKNIELD

(Roman

ROAD

Gypsy

LANE

44

38

A   B   Horsley
Lodge   C   D

21

row39

**HORSLEY LODGE
GOLF COURSE**

Park

Horsley
Lodge

Range

Club

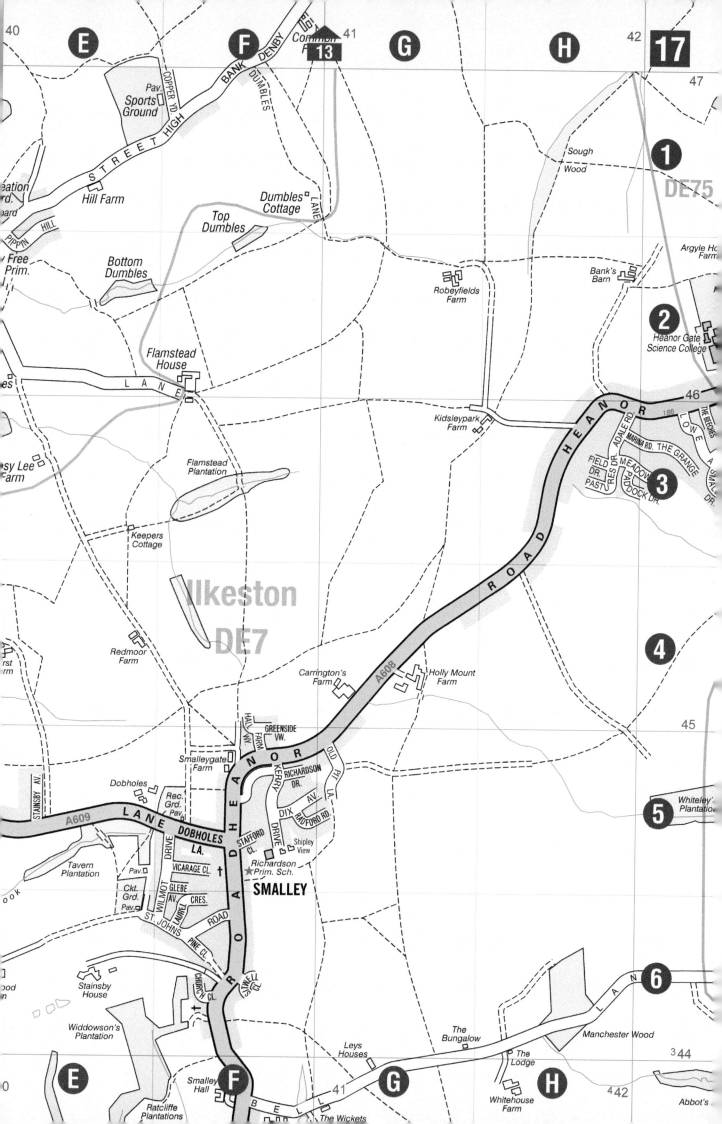

18 4 32

A   B   33   C   D

Cemetery

3 44

River

Ecclesbourne

Duffield
Meadows

Meadows
Farm

1

Weir

ECCLESBOURNE

SEFTON WAY

CEDAR DR.

MOULBOURN DR.

Rec. G

Mill G

SNAKE

MEADOWS

WILLIAM CL.

CORNHILL CL.

HOLL

DUFFIELD

Duffield
Meadows
Prim Sch

B5023

MEADOW FERRERS

Duffield
Meadows
Prim Sch

Meadows
Croft

FAIRLAWNS

ROAD

VALE

KIRKSW

BROOM CL.

SPRING-
FIELD DR.

HILL VIEW

PARK

Old

2

Spring
Carr

Tennis
Court

The
Kirkstyles

Farnah
House

ROAD

BDW

CURZON LA.

CAVEN-
DISH CL.

DEVON

43

Champion
Farm

CUMBERHILLS
GRANGE

3

CUMBERHILLS

Park
Leys

Celadon

Ireton
Rough

4

Cumberhill
Farm

ROAD

LANE

42

Botany
Farm

Reservoir

Gothic
Temple

BEECH

AVENUE

Park Nook
Farm

Park
Nook

Quarndon
Hill

Derby

The
Elms

5

Beech Avenue
Cottages

THE

Quarndon
House

ERHILLS

Park
Nook
House

Cricket
Field

Burley Wood

DLESTON

Stonequarry
Plantation

DE22

Pav.

The Plantation

6

North
Lodge

Park Nook
Wood

Quarndon Common

COMMON

COACH DR.

MONTPELIER

WOODLANDS

Holmwood Sel

41

King

A

B

22

33 QUAR C N

COMMON

ROAD

SINFIELDS

BURLEY

The Curzon
C of E
Prim. Sch.

D

32

Club
House

The Grange

Field Farm

Play

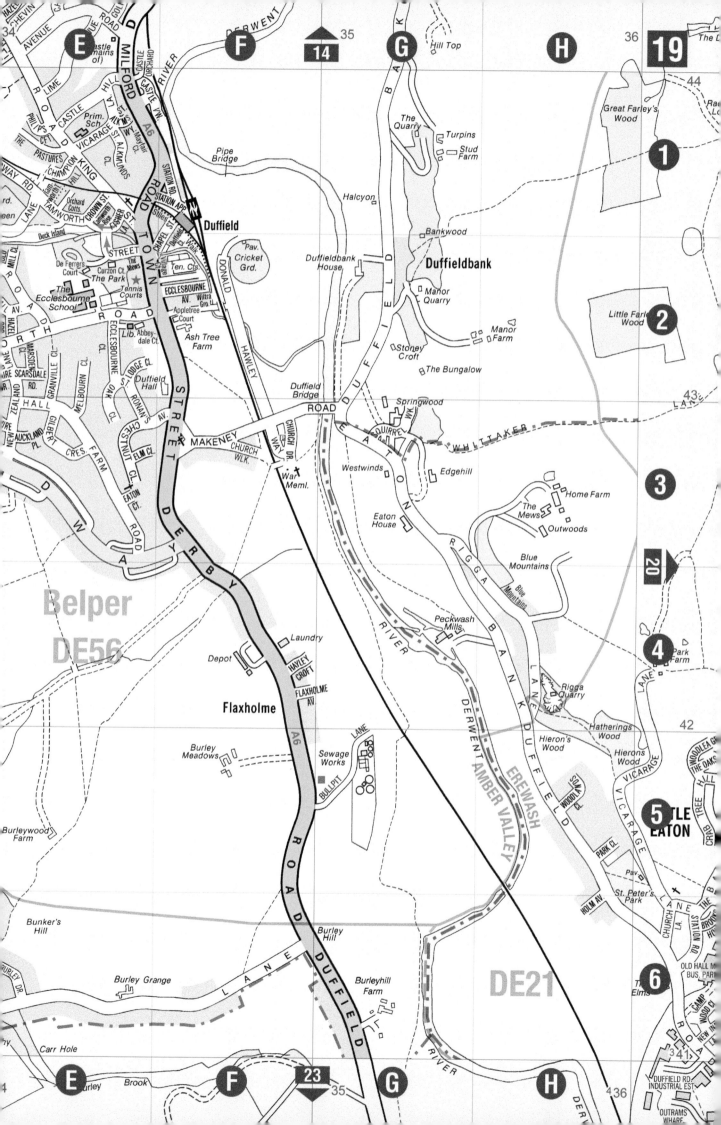

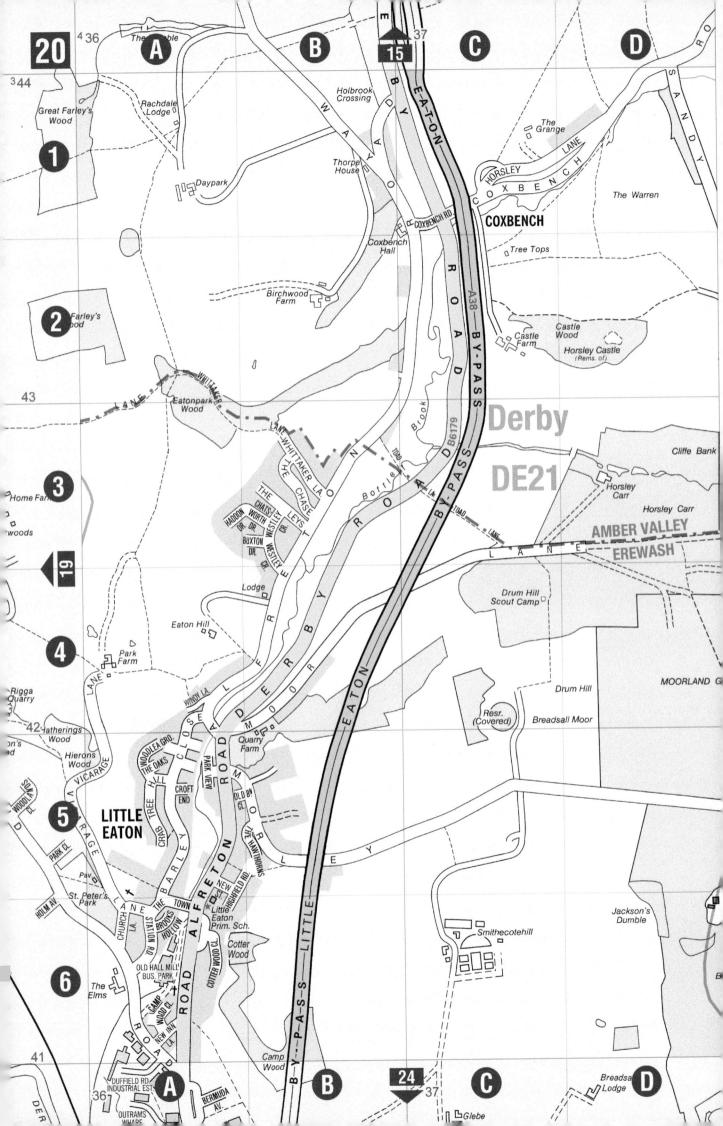

16

HORSLEY LODGE
GOLF COURSE

Horsley
Lodge

Driving
Range

Club
Ho.

Park

New
Plantation

Mill Brook

(Roman Road)

MILL

ROAD

Works

Woodside

HILLWOOD

WOODSIDE

1

2

43

Barn
Farm

Linkwood
Farm

Keepers
Covert

Abbott's Rough
Plantation

Horsley
Park Farm

Marks
Hill

Coppice
Dumble

Woodside
Farm

Cloves Hill
Farm

Yew
P

Brackley Gate
Farm

LANE

BRACKLEY

BRACKLEY GATE

GATE

CLOVES

S T R E E T

Dobb's Hill
Plantation

Moor
Plantation

ROAD

THE CROFT

The
Croft

Cloves
Wood

Cloves Wood

3

ROAD

Tudor
Lodge

Morley
Manor

Lodge

4

Quarry
Farm

Morleymoor
Farm

The Sycamores

**Ilkeston
DE7**

Driving
Range

Club
House

LF COURSE

QUARRY

BRICK

KILN

LANE

MAIN

The Tower
Course

5

42

Moor Side
Farm

Priory
Cottages

Top
Farm

Morley
Brickyards
Nature Reserve

Morley
Smithy

Morley Smithy
Farm

PRIMROSE DR.

LANE

Breadsall Priory Hotel
Golf and Country Club

ROAD

MORLEY ALMSHOUSES LA.

Lodge

Lodge
Farm

Morleymoor

Morley
Primary School

6

The
Gripps

ADSALL PRIORY
OLF COURSE

The
Wilderness

Morley House
Farm

Morley
Hall

CHURCH

ROAD

341

Morley Great &
Church

Church
Farm

CH

25

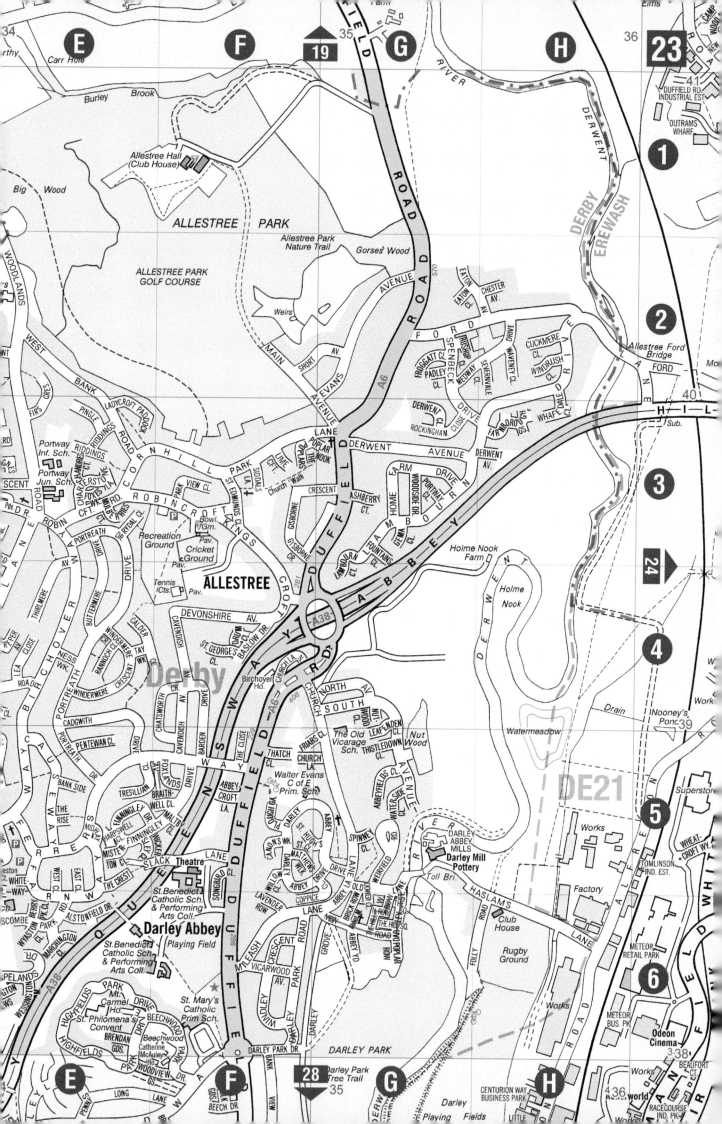

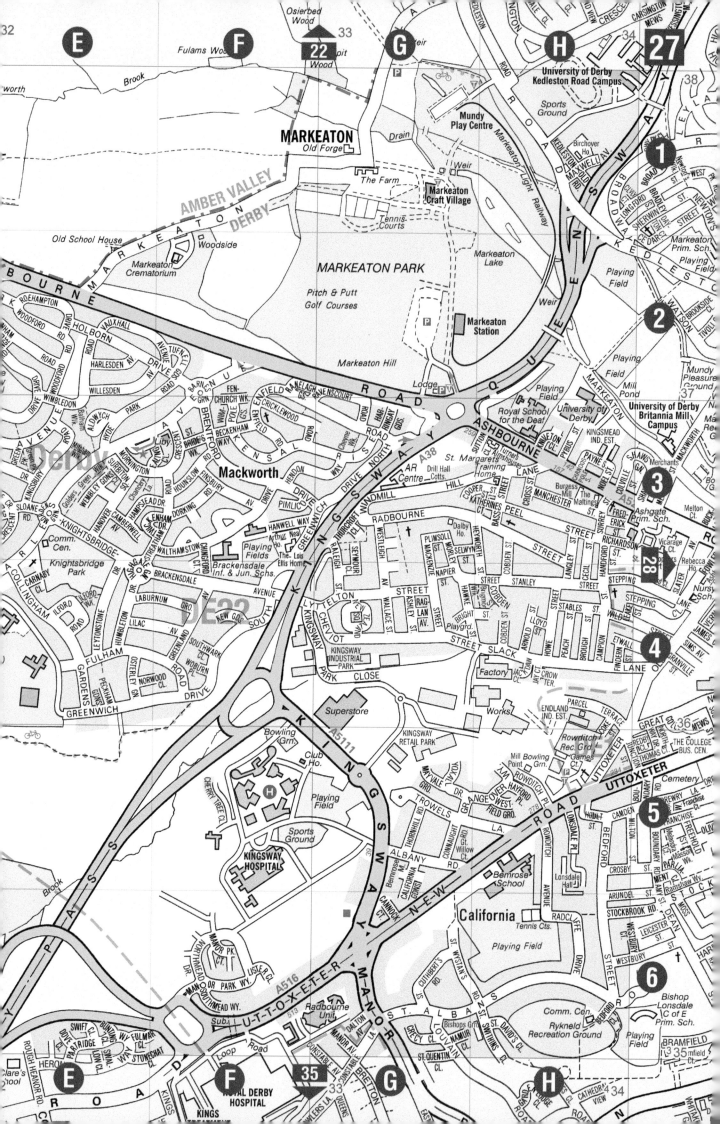

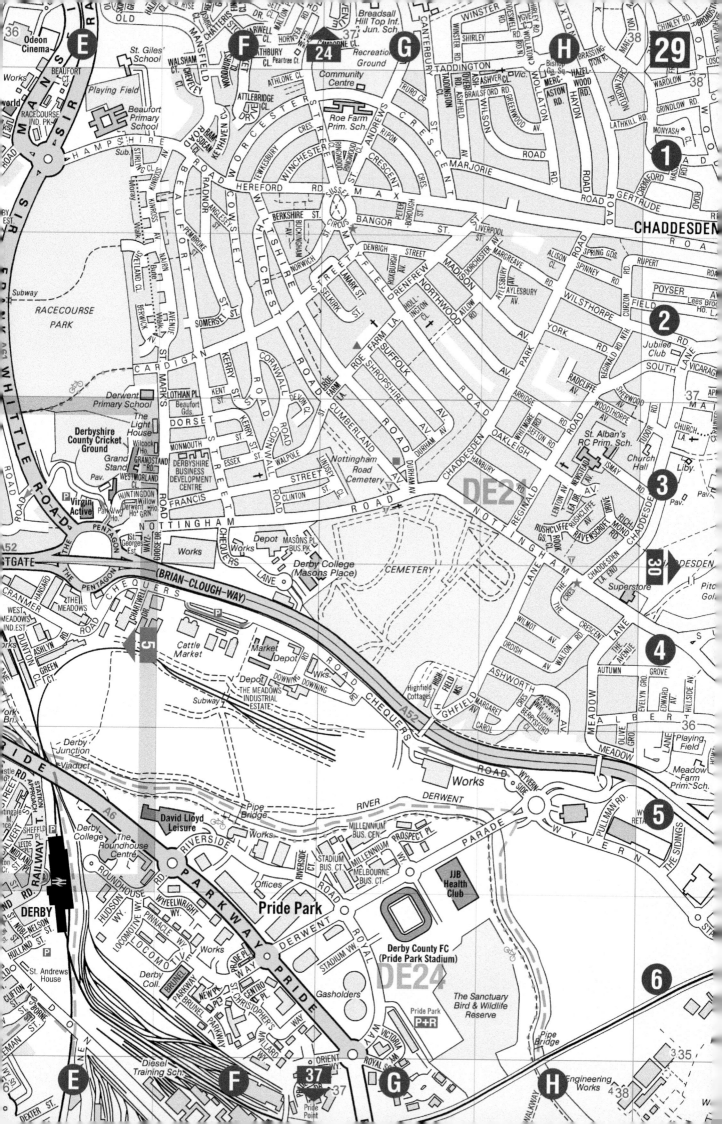

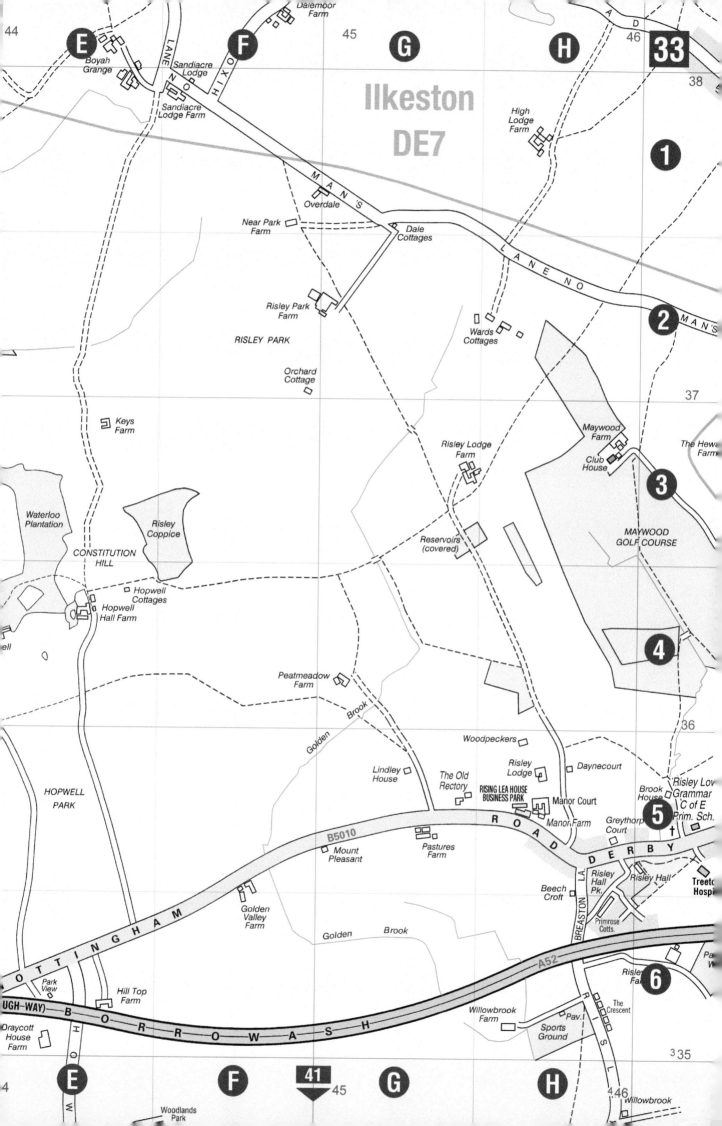

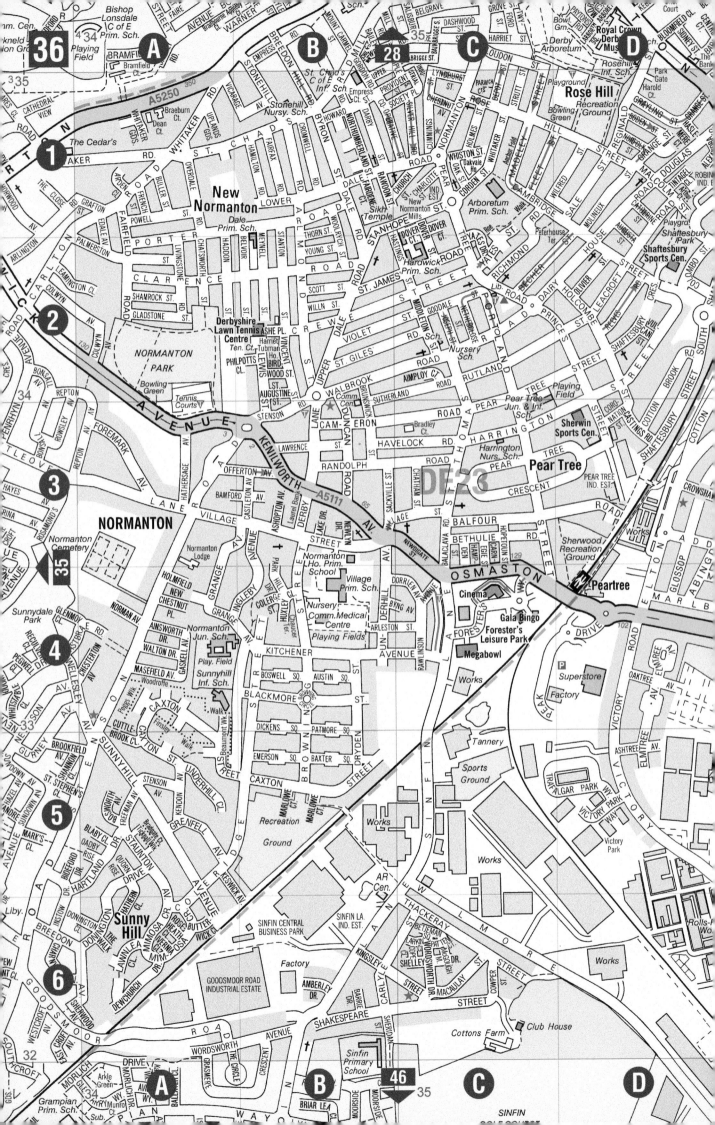

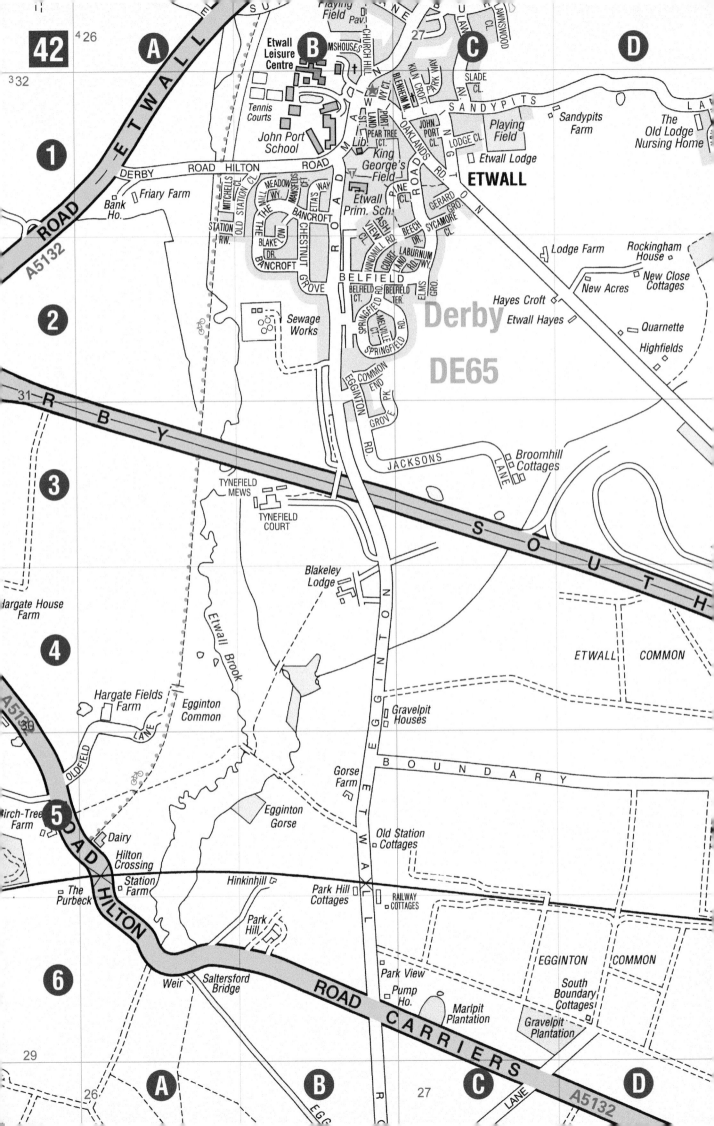

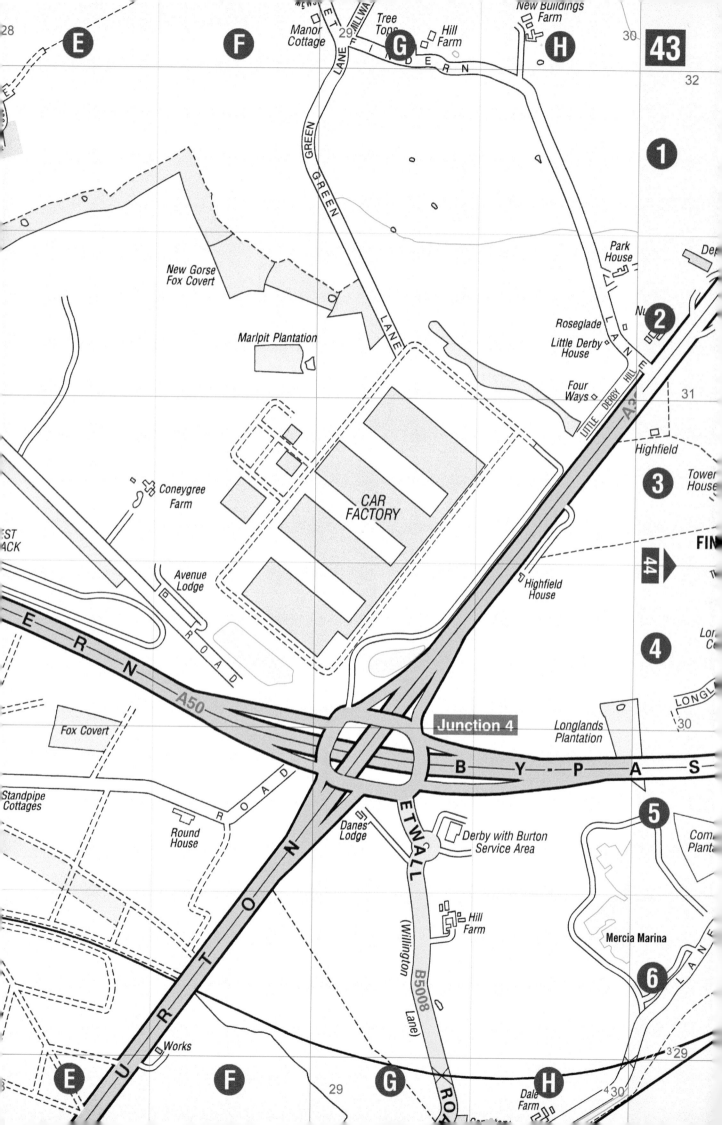

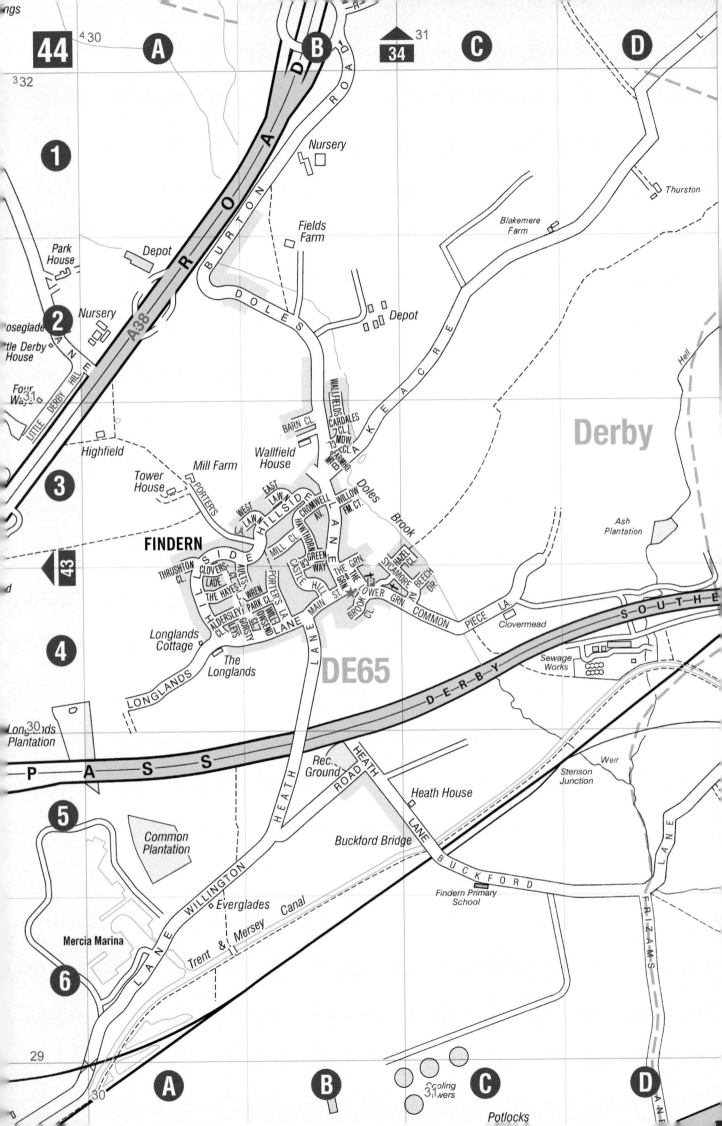

44

A **B** **C** **D**

1

2

3

4

5

6

Park House

Depot

Nursery

Roseglade

Little Derby House

Four Ways

Highfield

Tower House

Mill Farm

Wallfield House

FINDERN

Thrushton Cl.

Clovers Cl.

Lade

The Hayes

Aldersley Cl.

Longlands Cottage

The Longlands

Longlands Plantation

Nursery

Fields Farm

Depot

Wallfields Cl.

Cardales Cl.

Barn Cl.

East Law

West Law

Hillside

Cromwell Av.

Hawthorn Cl.

Mill Cl.

Green-way

The Grn.

Willow Fm. Ct.

Doles Brook

Hazel Cl.

Sycamore Av.

Beech Dr.

Wren Park Cl.

Townsend Cl.

Gorsty Leys

Castle Hill

Porter's Lane

Main Lane

Brook St.

Lower Grn.

Grn. Common

Piece La.

Clovermead

Longlands

Common Plantation

Willington Lane

Everglades

Mercia Marina

Trent & Mersey Canal

Rec. Ground

Heath Road

Heath Lane

Buckford Bridge

Buckford Lane

Findern Primary School

Heath House

Sewage Works

Weir

Stenson Junction

Frizams Lane

Derby

Blakemere Farm

Ash Plantation

Thurston

Hell

DE65

SOUTHE

DERBY

PASS

43

Potlocks

Cooling Towers

A B C D

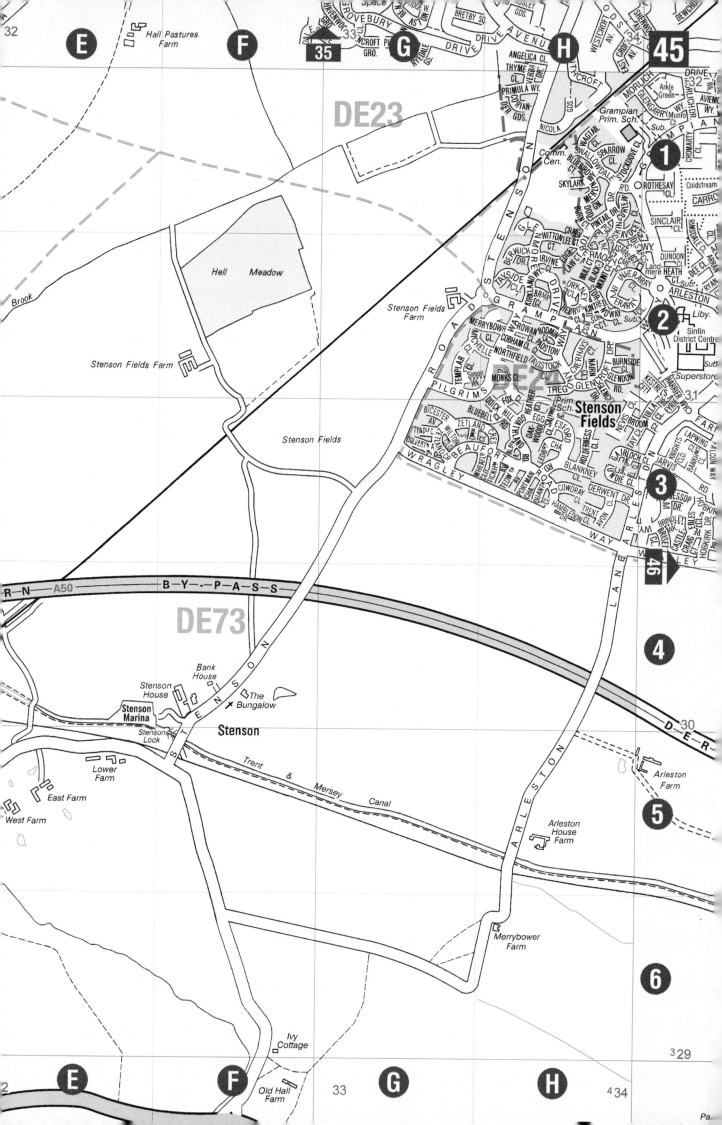

49

Junction 2

DE72

THULSTON

ASTON-ON-TRENT

Derby

E F 39 G H

E F G H

49

1 2 3 4 5 6

40 42

32

31

30

29

41

Sub.

DERBY SOUTHERN A6 BY-PASS

B5010

CHELLASTON LANE

AMBASTON LANE

AMBASTON

Ambaston Lane Farm

OAK RD
HANS LYNNOR CL
BROAD RD
GROVE
EBOR STURGES GROVE LA
CL
THE PINFOLD
YEW TREE
B5010 ROAD
BROAD LANE

Grange Farm

Grove Farm

Thurlestone Grange

White Lodge

DERBY ROAD

A50

50

R-B

Foxcovert Farm

Brickyard Plantation

Glebe Farm

ton Moor

Bird's Nest Farm

HILLCREST
ALDERSLADE CL.

Toadhole Plantation

Astonhill Farm

ASTON HILL

The Knob

Corners

HANGER BANK
Cemy.
THE LAWNS

MOOR LANE

DERBY LANE

MOORSIDE

5

BIG ROAD

Aston-on-Trent Prim. Sch.

AVENUE
COMPTON LANE
HOLDEN AV.
GREEN LEAS
LONG CROFT

OLD SCH. M.
WALNUT CL.
CLARKES
Manor Farm M.
CLARKES LA.
MANOR
GRN.
ASH CL.
WILLOW CL.
FARM

MANOR FARM RD.
Little Moorside

ROAD

WESTON ROAD
ELLISON AV.
VALERIE RD.
BELL AV.
HILTON GDNS
POSEY LA.
Rectory Mews
PARK VW.
Rectory Gds.
Lodge Mews
SHIRLEY PK.
Playing Field
Pavilion

ASTON HALL DR.
SHARDLOW

6

ROAD
WILLOW
CEDAR CFT.
MAPLE AV.
YATES
LAUREL DR.
BAY CL.
PARK DRIVE
HOLLY CT.
MULBERRY WY.
WAY

Birdcage Wood

442

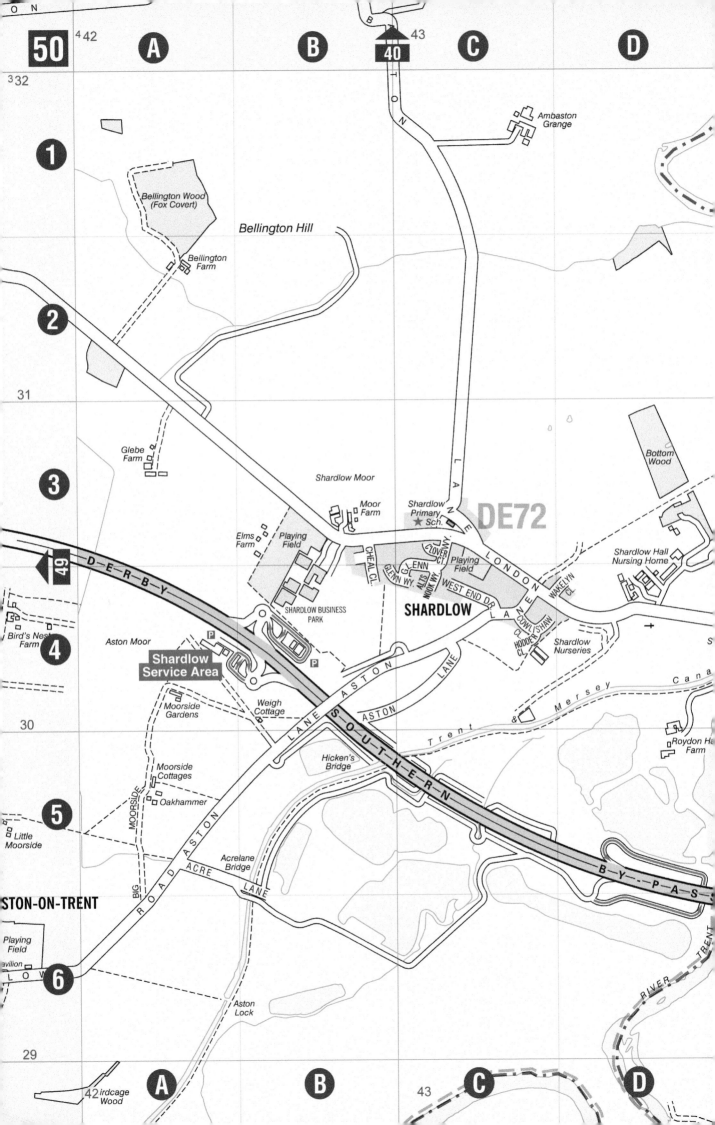

Sawley Grange

32

Ivy House Farm

1

St. Chads Water

ROAD

Weir

WILNE MILL

Wilne Bridge

WILNE

RIVER   DERWENT

2

EREWASH
SOUTH DERBYSHIRE

31

Aqueduct

Great Wilne

RIVER

Derby

LONG ROW

CAVENDISH CL.

THE WHARF

WILNE LANE

MILLFIELD

Playing Field

THE WHARF

Mill Green

P

Sewage Works

Derwent Mouth Lock

Porter's Bridge

Long Horse Bridge

3

ROAD

CANAL BANK

Shardlow Heritage Centre

dlow ck

CAVENDISH CT.

LONDON LANE

Shardlow Marina

RIVER TRENT

SOUTH DERBYSHIRE
NORTH WEST LEICESTERSHIRE

TAMWORTH

4

The Cottage

30

Cavendish Bridge

LANE

Depot

5

Cavendish Bridge

LANE BACK

ct

Ford

LANE

ROAD

Junction 1

RYCROFT

ROAD

6

A50

DONINGTON ROAD

DE74

TAMWORTH ROAD

329

BROAD   END   DARY   CT.   LONG AC   REDWING

Hemington Hole

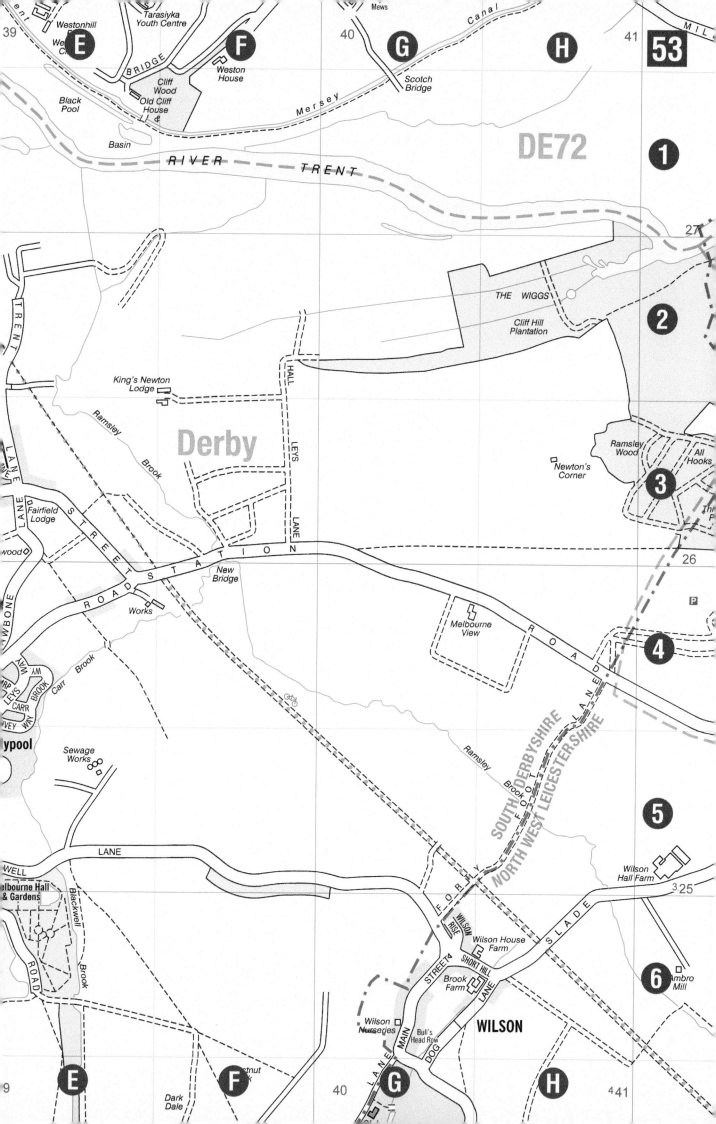

INDEX

Including Streets, Places & Areas, Hospitals etc., Industrial Estates,
Selected Flats & Walkways, Service Areas, Stations and Selected Places of Interest.

HOW TO USE THIS INDEX

1. Each street name is followed by its Postcode District, then by its Locality abbreviation(s) and then by its map reference;
   e.g. **Abbey Hill** DE22: Darl A..........**4G 23** is in the DE22 Postcode District and the Darley Abbey Locality and is to be found in square 4G on page **23**.
   The page number is shown in bold type.

2. A strict alphabetical order is followed in which Av., Rd., St., etc. (though abbreviated) are read in full and as part of the street name;
   e.g. **Ash Cres.** appears after **Ashcombe Gdns.** but before **Ashcroft Cl.**

3. Streets and a selection of flats and walkways that cannot be shown on the mapping, appear in the index with the thoroughfare to which they are connected shown in brackets;
   e.g. **Abbeydale Wlk.** DE24: A'ton..........5D **38** *(off Elvaston La.)*

4. Addresses that are in more than one part are referred to as not continuous.

5. Places and areas are shown in the index in BLUE TYPE and the map reference is to the actual map square in which the town centre or area is located and not to the place name shown on the map; e.g. ALLESTREE..........3F 23

6. An example of a selected place of interest is **Matthew Kirtley Mus.**..........3G 9

7. An example of a station is Belper Station (Rail)..........5B 10, also included is Park & Ride
   e.g. Meteor Centre Park & Ride..........6A 24

8. Service Areas are shown in the index in BOLD CAPITAL TYPE; e.g. **SHARDLOW SERVICE AREA** 4B **50**

9. An example of a Hospital or selected Healthcare facility is **BABINGTON HOSPITAL**..........1B 14

10. Map references for entries that appear on large scale page **4 & 5** are shown first, with small scale map references shown in brackets;
    e.g. **Abbotts Barn Cl.** DE22: Derb..........5B **4** (5B **28**)

GENERAL ABBREVIATIONS

All. : Alley	**Ct.** : Court	**Ho.** : House	**Pk.** : Park
App. : Approach	**Cres.** : Crescent	**Ho's.** : Houses	**Pl.** : Place
Arc. : Arcade	**Cft.** : Croft	**Ind.** : Industrial	**Ri.** : Rise
Av. : Avenue	**Dr.** : Drive	**Info.** : Information	**Rd.** : Road
Bk. : Back	**E.** : East	**La.** : Lane	**Sth.** : South
Bri. : Bridge	**Ent.** : Enterprise	**Lit.** : Little	**Sq.** : Square
Bldgs. : Buildings	**Est.** : Estate	**Lwr.** : Lower	**St.** : Street
Bus. : Business	**Fld.** : Field	**Mnr.** : Manor	**Ter.** : Terrace
Cen. : Centre	**Flds.** : Fields	**Mkt.** : Market	**Trad.** : Trading
Chyd. : Churchyard	**Gdn.** : Garden	**Mdw.** : Meadow	**Up.** : Upper
Circ. : Circle	**Gdns.** : Gardens	**Mdws.** : Meadows	**Va.** : Vale
Cir. : Circus	**Ga.** : Gate	**M.** : Mews	**Vw.** : View
Cl. : Close	**Gt.** : Great	**Mt.** : Mount	**Vis.** : Visitors
Comn. : Common	**Grn.** : Green	**Mus.** : Museum	**Wlk.** : Walk
Cnr. : Corner	**Gro.** : Grove	**Nth.** : North	**W.** : West
Cotts. : Cottages	**Hgts.** : Heights	**Pde.** : Parade	**Yd.** : Yard

LOCALITY ABBREVIATIONS

Allen : **Allenton**	Darl A : **Darley Abbey**	Losc : **Loscoe**	Ris : **Risley**
Alles : **Allestree**	Denb : **Denby**	Low H : **Lower Hartshay**	Shard : **Shardlow**
A'ton : **Alvaston**	Derb : **Derby**	Low K : **Lower Kilburn**	Shel L : **Shelton Lock**
Amb : **Ambaston**	Dray : **Draycott**	Mack : **Mackworth**	Sinf : **Sinfin**
Ash : **Ashbourne**	Duff : **Duffield**	Map : **Mapleton**	Smal : **Smalley**
Ast T : **Aston-on-Trent**	Egg : **Egginton**	Mare : **Marehay**	Spon : **Spondon**
Bar : **Bargate**	Elv : **Elvaston**	Mark : **Markeaton**	Stant B : **Stanton by Bridge**
Barr T : **Barrow upon Trent**	Etwa : **Etwall**	Mel : **Melbourne**	Sten : **Stenson**
Belp : **Belper**	Find : **Findern**	Mick : **Mickleover**	Sten F : **Stenson Fields**
Borr : **Borrowash**	Heag : **Heage**	Mil : **Milford**	Swan : **Swanwick**
Bread : **Breadsall**	Hem : **Hemington**	Mor : **Morley**	Swark : **Swarkestone**
Breas : **Breaston**	Hilt : **Hilton**	Neth H : **Nether Heage**	Thul : **Thulston**
Burn : **Burnaston**	Hol : **Holbrook**	Oak : **Oakwood**	Twy : **Twyford**
Cas D : **Castle Donington**	Hors : **Horsley**	Ockb : **Ockbrook**	West T : **Weston-on-Trent**
Chad : **Chaddesden**	Hors W : **Horsley Woodhouse**	Os'tn : **Osmaston**	Will : **Willington**
Chell : **Chellaston**	Kil : **Kilburn**	Pent : **Pentrich**	Wils : **Wilson**
Clif : **Clifton**	King N : **King's Newton**	Quarn : **Quarndon**	Yeld : **Yeldersley**
Cod : **Codnor**	Kir L : **Kirk Langley**	Radb : **Radbourne**	
Cox : **Coxbench**	Lit E : **Little Eaton**	Ridd : **Riddings**	
Dale A : **Dale Abbey**	Litt : **Littleover**	Rip : **Ripley**	

A

Abbey Cres. DE5: Rip 2E 13
Abbeycroft La. DE22: Darl A 5F 23
Abbeydale Cl. DE56: Kil.....................4B 16
Abbeydale Ct. DE56: Duff...................2E 19
Abbeydale Wlk. DE24: A'ton 5D 38
....(off Elvaston La.)
Abbeyfields Cl. DE22: Darl A.............5G 23
Abbey Hill DE22: Darl A......................4G 23
Abbey Hill Rd. DE22: Alles................5D 22
Abbey La. DE22: Darl A......................6G 23
Abbey St. DE22: Derb.........................6B 28
Abbey Yd. DE22: Darl A.....................6G 23
Abbot Cl. DE21: Oak..........................5C 24
Abbot M. DE22: Darl A........................6G 23
Abbots Gro. DE56: Belp.....................4C 10
Abbotts Barn Cl. DE22: Derb... 5B 4 (5B 28)
Abells DE5: Denb...............................2C 16
Abels Mill DE1: Derb.................2A 4 (3B 28)
....(off Brookbridge Ct.)
Aberdare Cl. DE21: Oak 5F 25
Abingdon Bus. Cen. DE24: Derb 2E 37

Abingdon St. DE24: Derb 4D 36
Abney Cl. DE3: Mick...........................1D 34
Acacia Av. DE3: Mick 2C 34
Acacia Cft. DE56: Belp......................1D 14
Acacia Dr. DE73: Mel.........................4C 52
Acer Cft. DE21: Oak...........................4C 24
Acorn Cl. DE24: Shel L.......................2G 47
Acorn Dr. DE56: Belp.........................4C 10
Acorn Way DE21: Chad......................6G 25
Acorn Way DE56: Belp.......................4C 10
Acrefield Way DE73: Chell.................3B 48
Acre La. DE72: Ast T..........................5A 50
Acresview Cl. DE22: Alles.................3D 22
Acton Rd. DE22: Mack........................3D 26
Adale Rd. DE7: Smal..........................3H 17
Addison Rd. DE24: Derb.....................3D 36
Adelaide Cl. DE3: Mick.......................5C 26
Adelphi Cl. DE23: Litt........................5E 35
Adler Ct. DE1: Derb............................2D 28
Adrian St. DE24: Derb........................5F 37
Adwick Cl. DE3: Mick.........................1A 34
Agard St. DE1: Derb.................2A 4 (3B 28)
Aimploy Ct. DE23: Derb......................2C 36

Ainley Cl. DE24: A'ton 4H 37
Ainsworth Dr. DE23: Derb 4A 36
Airedale Wlk. DE24: A'ton.................5C 38
Airfield Ind. Est. DE6: Ash..................5F 7
Albany Rd. DE22: Derb.......................5G 27
Albemarle Rd. DE21: Chad.................2B 30
Albert Cres. DE21: Chad....................5B 30
Albert Rd. DE21: Chad.......................4H 29
Albert Rd. DE5: Rip............................5C 8
Albert Rd. DE72: Breas......................4F 41
Albert St. DE1: Derb 4D 4 (4C 28)
Albert St. DE5: Rip.............................6E 9
Albert St. DE56: Belp.........................5B 10
Albion St. DE1: Derb 4D 4 (4C 28)
Albion St. DE5: Rip.............................6E 9
Albrighton Av. DE24: Sten F..............3H 45
Alder Cl. DE21: Oak...........................4C 24
Alderfen Cl. DE24: Shel L..................2F 47
Alderley Ct. DE21: Oak......................5E 25
Alder Rd. DE56: Belp.........................6C 10
Aldersgate DE22: Mack......................2D 26
Alderslade Cl. DE72: Ast T 4H 49
Aldersley Cl. DE65: Find....................4A 44

Alder Wlk. DE23: Derb........................6C 28
Aldwych DE22: Mack 3E 27
Alexandra Gdns. DE23: Derb.............1D 36
Alexandra Mills DE1: Derb.......4A 4 (4B 28)
....(off Gt. Northern Rd.)
Alexandre Cl. DE23: Litt.....................5H 35
Alfred Rd. DE56: Kil............................3A 16
Alfred St. DE5: Rip..............................5E 9
Alfreton Rd. DE21: Bread...................4A 24
Alfreton Rd. DE21: Derb....................1D 28
Alfreton Rd. DE21: Lit E.....................4A 24
Alfreton Rd. DE5: Cod 1H 13
Alice St. DE1: Derb...................2E 5 (3D 28)
Alison Cl. DE21: Chad.........................2H 29
Allan Av. DE23: Litt.............................3C 34
Allen St. DE24: Allen..........................6G 37
ALLENTON...6G 37
ALLESTREE...3F 23
Allestree Cl. DE24: A'ton...................3G 37
Allestree La. DE22: Alles...................5D 22
Allestree Pk. Golf Course 2F 23
Allestree St. DE24: A'ton...................3G 37
Allissa Av. DE5: Rip...........................2E 13

Belgrave St. – Brookvale Av.

Belgrave St. DE23: Derb.....6C 28
Bell Av. DE72: Ast T.....6G 49
Belle Acre Cl. DE56: Belp.....6B 10
Belle Vue Av. DE5: Mare.....4C 12
Belle Vue Rd. DE6: Ash.....3B 6
Belle Vue Ter. DE72: Borr.....2H 39
Bellingham Ct. DE22: Alles.....5C 22
Bell La. DE7: Smal.....6F 17
Belmont Dr. DE72: Borr.....1H 39
BELPER.....6B 10
Belper Adult Education Cen......1B 14
Belper Ho. DE21: Spon.....6E 31
Belper Leisure Cen......5F 11
Belper Pk. Local Nature Reserve.....6C 10
Belper River Gdns......4B 10
Belper Rd. DE1: Derb.....1B 28
Belper Rd. DE56: Bar.....2E 15
Belper Rd. DE56: Hol.....2E 15
Belper Rd. DE56: Kil.....1G 15
.....(not continuous)
Belper Rd. DE6: Ash.....3D 6
Belper St John's Chapel Heritage Cen......5C 10
Belper Station (Rail).....5B 10
Belrope Acre DE56: Belp.....1D 14
Belsize Cl. DE22: Mack.....3D 26
Belton Dr. DE5: Rip.....6E 9
Belvedere Cl. DE3: Mick.....5B 26
Belvoir Cl. DE72: Breas.....4G 41
Belvoir St. DE23: Derb.....2B 36
Bembridge Dr. DE24: A'ton.....6C 38
Bemrose M. DE22: Derb.....5G 27
Bemrose Rd. DE24: Allen.....4G 37
Benbow Av. DE73: Mel.....4C 52
Bendall Grn. DE23: Litt.....6G 35
Benjamin Outram Bus. Cen. DE5: Rip.....2E 13
Benmore Ct. DE21: Oak.....4F 25
Bennett St. DE24: Allen.....6F 37
Bensley Cl. DE73: Chell.....4A 48
Benson St. DE24: A'ton.....4H 37
Bentley St. DE24: Allen.....5G 37
Beresford Av. DE6: Ash.....2E 7
Beresford Dr. DE21: Spon.....5E 31
Berkeley Cl. DE23: Litt.....4H 35
Berkshire St. DE21: Chad.....1F 29
Bermuda Av. DE21: Lit E.....1A 24
Bernard Boam Dwellings DE5: Rip.....1D 12
.....(off Cedar Av.)
Bernard Gadsby Cl. DE6: Ash.....3B 6
Berry Pk. Cl. DE22: Darl A.....6E 23
Berwick Av. DE21: Chad.....2E 29
Berwick Cl. DE24: A'ton.....6B 38
Berwick Dr. DE24: Sten F.....2H 45
Bessalone Dr. DE56: Belp.....3C 10
Besthorpe Cl. DE21: Oak.....6F 25
Bethulie Rd. DE23: Derb.....3C 36
Betjeman Sq. DE24: Sinf.....6C 36
Beverley St. DE24: Derb.....1F 37
Bewdley Cl. DE73: Chell.....2A 48
Bexhill Wlk. DE21: Chad.....6C 24
Bicester Av. DE24: Sten F.....3G 45
Bickley Moss DE21: Oak.....6F 25
Bideford Cl. DE5: Rip.....5C 8
Bideford Dr. DE23: Derb.....5H 35
Big Moorside DE72: Ast T.....5A 50
Bilberry Cl. DE21: Oak.....6D 24
Bingham St. DE24: Allen.....5G 37
Binscombe La. DE21: Oak.....4D 24
Birch Cl. DE21: Spon.....3G 31
Birch Cl. DE5: Rip.....1D 12
Birches Rd. DE22: Alles.....4D 22
Birches Ter. DE6: Ash.....3C 6
Birchfield Cl. DE73: Chell.....3H 47
Birchover Ho. DE22: Darl A.....4F 23
Birchover Ho. DE22: Mark.....1H 27
Birchover Ri. DE21: Chad.....6D 24
Birchover Way DE22: Alles.....6C 22
Birch Va. DE56: Belp.....4B 10
Birchview Cl. DE56: Belp.....1D 14
Birchway Gro. DE23: Litt.....5E 35
Birchwood Av. DE23: Litt.....5H 35
Birchwood Vw. DE6: Ash.....1D 6
Birdcage Wlk. DE22: Mack.....3C 26
.....(not continuous)
Birdwood St. DE23: Derb.....2B 36
Birkbeck Cl. DE3: Mick.....6D 26
Birkdale Cl. DE3: Mick.....1E 35
Biscay Ct. DE21: Oak.....5G 25
Bishop Ga. Sq. DE21: Chad.....6D 24
Bishop Lonsdale Way DE3: Mick.....1D 34
Bishops Cl. DE5: Rip.....1E 13
Bishops Ct. DE73: Mel.....5D 52
Bishop's Dr. DE21: Oak.....5B 24
Bishops Grn. DE22: Derb.....6G 27
Blaby Cl. DE23: Derb.....5A 36
Blackberry Way DE56: Kil.....1H 15
Blackbird Row DE56: Bar.....2E 15
Blackden Cl. DE56: Belp.....5G 11
Blackmore St. DE23: Derb.....4B 36
Blackmount Ct. DE24: Sinf.....2H 45
Blacksmith Cft. DE5: Rip.....2D 12
Blackthorn Cl. DE21: Oak.....5C 24
Blackthorn Cl. DE73: Mel.....4C 52
Blackthorne Cl. DE56: Kil.....1H 15
Blackwell La. DE73: Mel.....5D 52
Blagreaves Av. DE23: Litt.....6G 35
Blagreaves La. DE23: Litt.....4G 35
Blakebrook Dr. DE73: Chell.....2A 48
Blakelow Dr. DE65: Etwa.....2B 42
Blakemore Av. DE73: Mel.....4D 52
Blakeney Ct. DE21: Oak.....6G 25
Blanch Cft. DE73: Mel.....5C 52
Blandford Cl. DE24: A'ton.....5D 38
Blankney Cl. DE24: Sten F.....3H 45
Blencathra Dr. DE3: Mick.....3C 34
Blenheim Ct. DE56: Belp.....4F 11
Blenheim Dr. DE22: Alles.....4C 22
Blenheim M. DE65: Etwa.....1C 42
Blenheim Pde. DE22: Alles.....3D 22
Blenheim Rd. DE6: Ash.....4F 7
Blind La. DE72: Breas.....3H 41
Blithfield Gdns. DE73: Chell.....3A 48
Bloomfield Cl. DE1: Derb.....6D 28
Bloomfield St. DE1: Derb.....6D 28
Bloom St. DE1: Derb.....5D 4 (5C 28)
Blore Cl. DE6: Ash.....4E 7
Bluebell Cl. DE24: Sten F.....3G 45
Bluebird Ct. DE24: Sinf.....1H 45
Blue Mountains DE56: Duff.....4H 19
Blyth Pl. DE21: Chad.....6B 24
Bobbin Way DE56: Belp.....4D 10
Boden St. DE23: Derb.....1D 36
Bodmin Cl. DE24: Sten F.....2H 45
Bodmin Grn. DE24: A'ton.....5B 38
Bog La. DE73: Mel.....6A 52
Bold La. DE1: Derb.....3C 4 (4C 28)
Bolsover Cl. DE5: Rip.....6E 9
Bolton St. DE55: Swan.....1D 8
Bonchurch Cl. DE24: A'ton.....6C 38
Bond La. DE56: Heag.....1B 10
Bonnyrigg Dr. DE21: Oak.....5E 25
Bonsall Av. DE23: Derb.....2H 35
Bonsall Dr. DE3: Mick.....6C 26
Boothby Av. DE6: Ash.....2D 6
Booth Dr. DE6: Ash.....4D 6
Boothgate DE56: Belp.....2G 11
BOOTHGATE.....2G 11
Booth St. DE24: A'ton.....4H 37
.....(not continuous)
Booth St. DE5: Rip.....5E 9
Border Bank DE5: Mare.....3D 12
Border Cres. DE24: A'ton.....6A 38
BORROWASH.....1H 39
Borrowash Bri. DE72: Elv.....3G 39
Borrowash By-Pass DE21: Spon.....5D 30
Borrowash La. DE72: Elv.....5G 39
Borrowash Rd. DE21: Spon.....6F 31
Borrowfield Rd. DE21: Spon.....6E 31
Borrowfields DE72: Borr.....2H 39
Boscastle Rd. DE24: A'ton.....5B 38
Bosley M. DE56: Belp.....4B 10
Boston Cl. DE21: Chad.....3C 30
Boswell Ct. DE6: Ash.....2C 6
.....(off Union St.)
Boswell Sq. DE23: Derb.....4B 36
Bosworth Av. DE23: Derb.....5A 36
Bottle Brook DE5: Denb.....2B 16
BOULTON.....5A 38
Boulton Dr. DE24: A'ton.....5A 38
Boulton La. DE24: Allen.....6G 37
.....(not continuous)
Boulton La. DE24: A'ton.....6G 37
.....(not continuous)
Boundary Ct. DE74: Cas D.....6F 51
Boundary Rd. DE22: Derb.....5A 28
Boundary Rd. DE65: Egg.....5C 42
Bourne Sq. DE72: Breas.....3H 41
Bourne St. DE1: Derb.....6D 4 (5C 28)
Bowbank Cl. DE23: Litt.....5E 35
Bowbridge Av. DE23: Litt.....6G 35
Bower St. DE24: A'ton.....3H 37
Bowland Cl. DE3: Mick.....2C 34
Bowlees Ct. DE23: Litt.....4C 34
Bowler Dr. DE56: Kil.....4A 16
Bowler St. DE5: Rip.....2D 12
Bowling All. DE56: Heag.....2B 10
Bowmer Rd. DE24: Derb.....2G 37
Bown Cl. DE56: Kil.....3A 16
Boxmoor Cl. DE23: Litt.....4D 34
Boyd Gro. DE73: Chell.....5A 48
Boyer St. DE22: Derb.....6A 28
Boyer Wlk. DE22: Derb.....6B 28
Boylestone Rd. DE23: Litt.....6G 35
Brackens Av. DE24: A'ton.....5H 37
Brackensdale Av. DE22: Mack.....4F 27
Bracken's La. DE24: A'ton.....5G 37
Brackley Dr. DE21: Spon.....4E 31
Brackley Ga. DE21: Bread.....3E 21
Brackley Ga. DE7: Mor.....3F 21
Bracknell Dr. DE24: A'ton.....6H 37
Bradbourne Ct. DE22: Derb.....6A 28
Bradbury Cl. DE72: Borr.....2A 40
Bradgate Ct. DE23: Derb.....5A 36
Bradgate Dr. DE5: Rip Chadwick Gro.....6B 8
Bradgate Dr. DE5: Rip Kepple Ga.....1F 13
Bradgate Pk. Vw. DE73: Chell.....5H 47
Brading Cl. DE24: A'ton.....6D 38
Bradley Ct. DE23: Derb.....3C 36
Bradley Dr. DE56: Belp.....5D 10
Bradley St. DE22: Derb.....1A 28
Bradley Vw. DE6: Ash.....1E 7
Bradmoor Gro. DE73: Chell.....3B 48
Bradshaw Cft. DE56: Belp.....3A 10
Bradshaw Dr. DE56: Hol.....5E 15
Bradshaw Retail Pk......6E 5 (5C 28)
Bradshaw Way DE1: Derb.....6E 5 (5D 28)
Bradwell Cl. DE3: Mick.....2C 34
Bradwell Way DE56: Belp.....4D 10
Braeburn Ct. DE23: Derb.....1A 36
Braemar Cl. DE24: Sten F.....2H 45
Brafield Cl. DE56: Belp.....5F 11
Brailsford Rd. DE21: Chad.....1G 29
Braintree Cl. DE21: Chad.....5B 24
Braithwell Cl. DE22: Darl A.....5F 23
Brambleberry Ct. DE21: Oak.....4F 25
Bramble M. DE3: Mick.....2B 34
Bramble St. DE1: Derb.....4B 4 (4B 28)
Bramble Way DE56: Kil.....1H 15
Bramblewick Dr. DE23: Litt.....5E 35
Brambling Cres. DE3: Mick.....6A 34
Bramfield Av. DE22: Derb.....6A 28
Bramfield Ct. DE22: Derb.....6A 28
Bramley Cl. DE21: Oak.....4G 25
Brampton Cl. DE3: Mick.....6A 26
Brampton Ct. DE56: Belp.....5F 11
Brandelhow Ct. DE21: Oak.....4F 25
Branksome Av. DE24: A'ton.....4C 38
Brassington Rd. DE21: Chad.....6D 24
Brayfield Av. DE23: Litt.....3H 35
Brayfield Rd. DE23: Litt.....3G 35
Breach La. DE73: Mel.....3A 52
Breach Rd. DE5: Denb.....5F 13
BREADSALL.....3C 24
BREADSALL HILLTOP.....4C 24
Breadsall Priory Golf Course.....6E 21
BREASTON.....3H 41
Breaston Ind. Est. DE72: Breas.....4G 41
Breaston La. DE72: Ris.....6H 33
Brecon Cl. DE21: Spon.....3E 31
Breedon Av. DE23: Litt.....6H 35
Breedon Hill Rd. DE23: Derb.....6B 28
Brendan Gdns. DE22: Darl A.....6E 23
Brentford Dr. DE22: Mack.....3F 27
Bretby Sq. DE23: Litt.....6G 35
Bretton Av. DE23: Litt.....1G 35
Bretton Rd. DE56: Belp.....4G 11
Brewster Cl. DE55: Swan.....1D 8
Breydon Cl. DE24: Shel L.....1F 47
Brian Clough Way DE21: Chad.....3H 5 (4F 29)
Brian Clough Way DE21: Derb.....3H 5 (4F 29)
Brian Clough Way DE72: Ockb.....6G 31
Briar Cl. DE21: Chad.....5B 30
Briar Cl. DE72: Borr.....1A 40
Briar Lea Cl. DE24: Sinf.....1B 46
Briarsgate DE22: Alles.....5D 22
Briars La. DE23: Litt.....4E 35
.....(not continuous)
Briars Way DE5: Rip.....6D 8
Briarwood Way DE23: Litt.....5G 35
Brick Kiln La. DE7: Mor.....5F 21
Brick Row DE22: Darl A.....6G 23
Brick St. DE1: Derb.....3A 28
Brickyard Cotts. DE6: Ash.....4D 6
Brickyard La. DE5: Rip.....6F 9
Brickyard La. DE56: Kil.....1H 15
Bridge, The DE56: Mil.....4C 14
Bridge Fld. DE72: Breas.....4G 41
Bridge Foot DE56: Belp.....4A 10
Bridge Ga. DE1: Derb.....1C 4 (3C 28)
Bri. Hill DE56: Belp.....4A 10
BRIDGEHILL.....4A 10
Bridge La. DE72: West T.....1E 53
Bridgend Ct. DE21: Oak.....5G 25
Bridgeness Rd. DE23: Litt.....5D 34
Bridgeport Rd. DE21: Chad.....3C 30
Bridgeside Way DE21: Spon.....6D 30
Bridge St. DE1: Derb.....2A 4 (3B 28)
Bridge St. DE56: Belp.....5B 10
Bridge Vw. DE56: Mil.....4C 14
Bridge Yd. Av. DE5: Rip.....3E 9
Bridgwater Cl. DE24: A'ton.....4C 38
Bridle Cl. DE73: Chell.....5A 48
Bridle Ga. La. DE24: A'ton.....4D 38
Bridle La. DE5: Low H.....4A 8
Bridle La. DE5: Rip.....4D 8
Bridle La. DE56: Heag.....5A 8
Brierfield Way DE3: Mick.....2C 34
Brigden Av. DE24: Allen.....4G 37
Brighstone Cl. DE24: A'ton.....6C 38
Brighton Rd. DE24: A'ton.....2H 37
Bright St. DE22: Derb.....4G 27
Brightwater Cl. DE24: Shel L.....2G 47
Brigmor Wlk. DE22: Derb.....4H 27
Brindle Way DE23: Litt.....6E 35
Brindley Ct. DE24: Allen.....5G 37
Brindley Wlk. DE24: Sten F.....3A 46
Brisbane Rd. DE3: Mick.....5C 26
Briset Cl. DE24: Sten F.....3A 46
Bristol Dr. DE3: Mick.....1C 34
Britannia Av. DE5: Rip.....2G 13
Britannia Ct. DE1: Derb.....1D 4 (3C 28)
Brittain Dr. DE5: Rip.....6G 9
Broad Bank DE22: Derb.....1A 28
Broadfields Cl. DE22: Derb.....1B 28
Broad La. DE72: Thul.....1F 49
Broadleaf Cl. DE21: Oak.....5C 24
Broad Oak Cl. DE55: Swan.....1E 9
Broad Rushes DE74: Cas D.....6F 51
Broadstone Cl. DE21: Chad.....6E 25
Broadway DE22: Derb.....1H 27
Broadway DE5: Rip.....5E 9
Broadway DE56: Duff.....2D 18
Broadway Av. DE5: Rip.....6E 9
Broadway Ct. DE5: Rip.....5E 9
Broadway Dr. DE5: Rip.....6E 9
Broadway Pk. Cl. DE22: Derb.....1A 28
Brockley DE21: Spon.....4E 31
Brodie Cl. DE73: Chell.....3G 47
Bromley St. DE22: Derb.....2A 28
Brompton Rd. DE22: Mack.....3D 26
.....(not continuous)
Bromyard Dr. DE73: Chell.....2A 48
Bronte Pl. DE23: Litt.....3F 35
Brookbridge Ct. DE1: Derb.....2A 4 (3B 28)
Brook Cl. DE22: Quarn.....3C 22
Brook Cl. DE65: Find.....4B 44
Brookdale Dr. DE23: Litt.....6E 35
Brooke Cl. DE56: Belp.....6B 10
Brookfield Av. DE21: Chad.....1B 30
Brookfield Av. DE23: Derb.....5H 35
Brookfield Cl. DE5: Cod.....6H 9
Brookfields DE5: Low K.....4G 15
Brookfields Dr. DE21: Bread.....3B 24
Brook Gdns. DE1: Derb.....1A 4 (3A 28)
Brook Ho. DE1: Derb.....2A 4 (3B 28)
.....(off Brook St.)
Brookhouse St. DE24: Allen.....6F 37
Brooklands Dr. DE23: Litt.....3G 35
Brook La. DE5: Rip.....2D 12
Brook Rd. DE72: Borr.....2H 39
Brook Rd. DE72: Thul.....1F 49
Brooks Hollow DE21: Lit E.....6A 20
Brookside DE1: Derb.....1B 4 (3B 28)
Brookside DE56: Belp.....6B 10
Brookside DE6: Ash.....3E 7
.....(not continuous)
Brookside Cl. DE1: Derb.....2A 28
Brookside Mdws. DE6: Ash.....3F 7
Brookside Rd. DE21: Bread.....3B 24
Brook St. DE1: Derb.....1A 4 (3B 28)
Brook St. DE56: Heag.....2B 10
Brook St. DE56: Neth H.....1A 10
Brook St. DE75: Losc.....4H 13
Brookvale Av. DE5: Cod.....1H 13
Brookvale Av. DE5: Denb.....1A 16

Chester Grn. Rd. – Cumberland Av.

Chester Grn. Rd. DE1: Derb 2C **28**
(not continuous)
Chester Pk. DE21: Derb 1D **28**
Chesterton Av. DE23: Derb 4A **36**
Chesterton Rd. DE21: Spon 3E **31**
Chestnut Av. DE23: Derb 1C **36**
Chestnut Av. DE3: Mick 6B **26**
Chestnut Av. DE5: Rip 1D **12**
Chestnut Av. DE56: Belp 1C **14**
Chestnut Av. DE56: Hol 4E **15**
Chestnut Av. DE73: Chell 2H **47**
Chestnut Cl. DE56: Duff 3E **19**
Chestnut Cl. DE7: Hors W 4C **16**
Chestnut Dr. DE6: Ash 5E **7**
Chestnut Gro. DE65: Etwa 1B **42**
Chestnut Gro. DE72: Borr 6A **32**
Cheveley Ct. DE21: Chad 1F **29**
Cheverton Cl. DE24: A'ton 6D **38**
Chevin All. DE56: Mil 4C **14**
Chevin Av. DE3: Mick 1D **34**
Chevin Av. DE72: Borr 1A **40**
CHEVINEND 4A **14**
Chevin Golf Course 6A **14**
Chevin M. DE56: Belp 1B **14**
Chevin Pl. DE1: Derb 2B **28**
Chevin Rd. DE1: Derb 2B **28**
Chevin Rd. DE56: Duff 6A **14**
CHEVINSIDE 1A **14**
Chevin Va. DE56: Duff 6A **14**
Chevin Vw. DE56: Belp 5B **10**
Cheviot St. DE22: Derb 4G **27**
Cheyenne Gdns. DE21: Chad 4B **30**
Cheyne Wlk. DE22: Mack 3G **27**
Chilson Dr. DE3: Mick 6A **26**
Chime Cl. DE21: Oak 5C **24**
Chingford Ct. DE22: Mack 3F **27**
Chinley Rd. DE21: Chad 6E **25**
Chiswick Cl. DE22: Mack 3D **26**
Christchurch Ct. DE1: Derb 2D **4** (3C **28**)
Church Banks DE6: Ash 2C **6**
Church Cl. DE7: Smal 6F **17**
Church Cl. DE73: Chell 4A **48**
Church Ct. DE5: Denb 2D **16**
Church Cft. DE5: Rip 5D **8**
Churchdown Cl. DE21: Oak 5F **25**
Church Dr. DE56: Duff 3F **19**
Church Farm Rd. DE5: Rip 1E **13**
Church Hill DE21: Spon 5D **30**
Church Hill DE65: Etwa 1B **42**
Churchill Cl. DE72: Breas 3H **41**
Church La. DE21: Bread 3C **24**
Church La. DE21: Chad 3A **30**
Church La. DE21: Lit E 6A **20**
Church La. DE22: Darl A 4F **23**
Church La. DE22: Mack 1D **26**
Church La. DE56: Belp 5B **10**
Church La. DE7: Hors W 5D **16**
Church La. DE7: Mor 1G **25**
Church La. Nth. DE22: Darl A 4F **23**
Church M. DE21: Spon 5D **30**
Church Rd. DE22: Quarn 3C **22**
Churchside Wlk. DE22: Derb 5A **28**
Church Sq. DE73: Mel 6D **52**
Church St. DE5: Rip Cromford Rd. 5D **8**
Church St. DE5: Rip Orchard Cl. 2G **13**
Church St. DE21: Hors 5H **15**
Church St. DE21: Spon 5D **30**
Church St. DE23: Derb 1C **36**
Church St. DE23: Litt 2G **35**
Church St. DE24: A'ton 4C **38**
Church St. DE5: Denb 2D **16**
Church St. DE56: Belp 5C **10**
Church St. DE56: Heag 1A **10**
Church St. DE56: Hol 5E **15**
Church St. DE56: Kil 3H **15**
Church St. DE6: Ash 2C **6**
Church St. DE72: Ockb 5A **32**
Church St. DE73: Mel 5D **52**
Church Vw. DE56: Belp 5C **10**
Church Vw. DE6: Clif 6A **6**
Church Vw. DE72: Breas 4H **41**
Church Vw. DE75: Losc 5H **13**
Church Wlk. DE22: Alles 3F **23**
Church Wlk. DE23: Derb 6B **28**
Church Wlk. DE56: Belp 5B **10**
Church Wlk. DE56: Duff 3F **19**
CHURCH WILNE 6F **41**
Church Wilne Water Sports Club 6H **41**
CINDERHILL 1G **15**
Circle, The DE24: Sinf 6A **36**
City Ga. DE24: Derb 1F **37**
City Ga. Bus. Pk. DE24: Derb 1F **37**
City Rd. DE1: Derb 2C **28**
City Rd. Ind. Pk. DE1: Derb 2C **28**
City Wlk. DE1: Derb 1D **4** (3C **28**)
Clare Ho. DE1: Derb 6C **28**
Clarence Rd. DE23: Derb 2A **36**
Clarkes La. DE72: Ast T 5H **49**
Clarke St. DE1: Derb 1F **5** (3D **28**)
Clay St. DE72: Dray 4E **41**
Clement Rd. DE7: Hors W 4C **16**
Cleveland Av. DE21: Chad 4B **30**
Cleveland Av. DE72: Dray 4D **40**
Clifford St. DE24: Derb 1F **37**
CLIFTON 6A **6**
Clifton Dr. DE3: Mick 6C **26**
Clifton Rd. DE22: Alles 4D **22**
Clifton Rd. DE6: Ash 5A **6**
(not continuous)
Clifton Rd. DE6: Clif 5A **6**
(not continuous)
Clifton St. DE1: Derb 6E **29**
Clinton St. DE21: Chad 3F **29**
Clipstone Gdns. DE21: Oak 5F **25**
Clock Way DE21: Spon 6F **31**
Cloisters Ct. DE21: Oak 4D **24**
Close, The DE22: Darl A 5F **23**
Close, The DE23: Derb 1H **35**
Cloudwood Cl. DE23: Litt 2F **35**
Clovelly Ct. DE22: Derb 1H **27**
Clover Cl. DE21: Spon 4F **31**
Clover Ct. DE72: Shard 3C **50**
Cloverdale Dr. DE24: Sinf 3B **46**
Cloverslade DE65: Find 4A **44**
Cloves Hill DE7: Mor 3G **21**
Clumber Cl. DE5: Rip 6E **9**
Clumber Cl. DE6: Ash 4C **6**
Cluster Rd. DE56: Belp 5B **10**
Clusters Ct. DE56: Belp 5B **10**
Coach Dr. DE22: Quarn 6D **18**
Coachman's Cl. DE6: Ash 3C **6**
(off School La.)
Coach Rd. DE5: Rip Codnor La. 4H **9**
Coach Rd. DE5: Rip Derby Rd. 3E **9**
Coach Rd. DE5: Rip Nottingham Rd. 4F **9**
Cobden St. DE22: Derb 4H **27**
(not continuous)
Cobden St. DE5: Rip 5D **8**
Cobham Cl. DE24: Sten F 2H **45**
Cobthorne Dr. DE22: Alles 3C **22**
Coburn Pl. DE1: Derb 4B **4** (4B **28**)
Cockayne St. Nth. DE24: Allen 5G **37**
Cockayne St. Sth. DE24: Allen 5G **37**
Cock Hill DE6: Clif 6A **6**
Cock Pitt, The DE1: Derb 4E **5** (4D **28**)
Cockshut La. DE73: Mel 6B **52**
Cockshut La. Bus. Cen. DE73: Mel 5C **52**
Cod Beck Cl. DE24: A'ton 5C **38**
CODNOR 1H **13**
CODNOR BREACH 5G **13**
Codnor Denby La. DE5: Cod 5G **13**
Codnor Denby La. DE5: Denb 5G **13**
Codnor Ga. DE5: Cod 6H **9**
CODNOR GATE 6H **9**
Codnor Ga. Bus. Pk. DE5: Rip 6G **9**
Codnor Ga. Ind. Est. DE5: Rip 5H **9**
Codnor La. DE55: Ridd 4H **9**
Cokayne Av. DE6: Ash 2D **6**
Cokayne M. DE6: Ash 2D **6**
Coke St. DE1: Derb 4H **27**
Coldstream Wlk. DE24: Sinf 1A **46**
Cole La. DE72: Borr 5A **32**
Cole La. DE72: Ockb 5A **32**
Coleman St. DE24: A'ton 4G **37**
Coleraine Cl. DE21: Chad 5B **30**
Coleridge St. DE23: Derb 6A **36**
(not continuous)
Colin Av. DE5: Cod 1H **13**
College, The DE5: Denb 6B **12**
College Bus. Cen., The DE22: Derb 5A **28**
College Grn. Wlk. DE3: Mick 6D **26**
College M. DE1: Derb 4A **28**
College Pl. DE1: Derb 2C **4** (3C **28**)
Collier La. DE72: Ockb 5A **32**
Colliers Ct. DE5: Rip 2G **13**
Collingham Gdns. DE22: Mack 4E **27**
Collis Cl. DE24: Allen 4G **37**
Collumbell Av. DE72: Ockb 4A **32**
Colombo St. DE23: Derb 2D **36**
Coltsfoot Dr. DE24: Sinf 3B **46**
Columbine Cl. DE21: Oak 6E **25**
Colville St. DE22: Derb 3H **27**
Colwell Dr. DE24: A'ton 6C **38**
Colwyn Av. DE23: Derb 2H **35**
Colyear St. DE1: Derb 4C **4** (4C **28**)
Combined Court Derby 3E **5** (4D **28**)
Comfrey Cl. DE23: Litt 5D **34**
Commerce St. DE24: A'ton 3H **37**
Commerce St. DE73: Mel 5C **52**
Common, The DE22: Quarn 5B **18**
COMMON END 1B **34**
Common End DE65: Etwa 2B **42**
Common Piece La. DE65: Find 4C **44**
COMPTON 3D **6**
Compton Av. DE72: Ast T 5G **49**
Compton Cl. DE24: A'ton 5C **38**
Compton St. DE6: Ash 2D **6**
Coniston Av. DE21: Spon 3E **31**
Coniston Cres. DE21: Chad 5B **24**
Connaught Rd. DE22: Derb 5G **27**
Consett Cl. DE21: Chad 6B **24**
Consort Gdns. DE21: Oak 4G **25**
Constable Av. DE23: Litt 6G **27**
Constable Dr. DE23: Litt 1F **35**
Constable La. DE23: Litt 1G **35**
Convent of the Holy Name 5G **25**
Conway Av. DE72: Borr 1B **40**
Cook Cl. DE56: Belp 4G **11**
Cookfield DE56: Heag 1G **11**
Cookham Cl. DE3: Mick 1A **34**
Co-operative St. DE23: Derb 1B **36**
Cooper's Cl. DE6: Ash 2D **6**
Coopers Cl. DE72: Borr 2B **40**
Coopers Gdns. DE6: Ash 3C **6**
Cooper St. DE22: Derb 3G **27**
Cooper St. DE5: Rip 6D **8**
Copecastle Sq. DE1: Derb 5E **5** (4D **28**)
Cope Cl. DE24: Sinf 6C **36**
Copeland St. DE1: Derb 5F **5** (5D **28**)
Copeland Wlk. DE1: Derb 5E **5** (5D **28**)
Copes Way DE21: Chad 1A **30**
Copley Cft. DE6: Ash 1E **7**
Copper Beeches DE5: Rip 5C **8**
Copperleaf Cl. DE22: Derb 6A **4** (5B **28**)
Copper Yd. DE5: Denb 1F **17**
Coppice Cl. DE22: Darl A 6F **23**
Coppice Cl. DE56: Kil 3A **16**
Coppice End Rd. DE22: Alles 6C **22**
Coppice Pk. DE72: Dray 2C **40**
Coppicewood Dr. DE23: Litt 2E **35**
Copse Gro. DE23: Litt 4E **35**
Coral Cl. DE24: Derb 1G **37**
Corbel Cl. DE21: Oak 5C **24**
Corbridge Gro. DE23: Litt 4E **35**
Corby Cl. DE24: A'ton 6H **37**
Cordelia Way DE73: Chell 3G **47**
Corden Av. DE3: Mick 1E **35**
Corden St. DE23: Derb 1C **36**
Cordville Cl. DE21: Chad 4B **30**
Corfe Cl. DE23: Litt 5H **35**
Coriander Gdns. DE23: Litt 1H **45**
Corinium Cl. DE24: A'ton 6D **38**
Cornflower Dr. DE21: Oak 5E **25**
Cornhill DE22: Alles 3E **23**
Cornhill Cl. DE56: Duff 1D **18**
Corn Mkt. DE1: Derb 3D **4** (4C **28**)
Cornmill Cl. DE72: Elv 6D **38**
Cornwall Rd. DE21: Chad 2F **29**
Coronation Av. DE24: A'ton 6C **38**
Coronation Av. DE56: Belp 4C **10**
Coronation Cl. DE73: Mel 4C **52**
Coronation St. DE23: Derb 3D **36**
Coronet Ct. DE21: Oak 4H **25**
Corporation St. DE1: Derb 3D **4** (4C **28**)
Cotswold Cl. DE23: Litt 3G **35**
Cottage Cl. DE56: Heag 2G **11**
Cottage Ct. DE56: Belp 6G **11**
Cottisford Cl. DE23: Litt 3E **35**
Cotton Brook Rd. DE23: Derb 3D **36**
Cotton La. DE24: Derb 3D **36**
Countess Gro. DE73: Chell 5H **47**
Countisbury Dr. DE21: Oak 5E **25**
Coupe St. DE5: Rip 1F **13**
Court, The DE24: A'ton 5B **38**
Courtland Dr. DE24: A'ton 5A **38**
Courtland Gdns. DE24: A'ton 4B **38**
Courtland Rd. DE65: Etwa 2B **42**
Courtney Way DE56: Belp 4F **11**
Courtway Cres. DE73: Chell 4G **47**
Courtyard Pl. DE21: Spon 4E **31**
Covent Gdn. Cl. DE72: Borr 1H **39**
Coverdale Wlk. DE24: A'ton 5C **38**
(off Elvaston La.)
Covert, The DE21: Spon 5E **31**
Cowdray Cl. DE24: Sten F 3H **45**
COWHILL 1C **14**
Cowley St. DE1: Derb 2A **28**
Cowlishaw Cl. DE72: Shard 4C **50**
Cowper St. DE24: Sinf 6C **36**
Cowsley Rd. DE21: Chad 1F **29**
Cowslip Mdw. DE72: Dray 4F **41**
COXBENCH 1C **20**
Coxbench Rd. DE21: Cox 1C **20**
Coxbench Rd. DE21: Hors 1C **20**
Cox Grn. Ct. DE23: Litt 4D **34**
Coxon St. DE21: Spon 4E **31**
Crabtree Cl. DE22: Alles 3C **22**
Crab Tree Hill DE21: Lit E 5A **20**
Crabtree Hill DE22: Alles 3C **22**
Craddock Av. DE21: Spon 6E **31**
Craiglee Ct. DE24: Sinf 1H **45**
Cranberry Gro. DE23: Litt 5D **34**
Cranhill Cl. DE23: Litt 5D **34**
Cranmer Rd. DE21: Derb 3G **5** (4E **29**)
Cranwood Cl. DE24: Allen 6F **37**
Crawley Rd. DE24: A'ton 6H **37**
Crayford Rd. DE24: A'ton 6A **38**
Crecy Cl. DE22: Derb 6G **27**
Crescent, The DE21: Chad 4H **29**
Crescent, The DE24: A'ton 5G **37**
Crescent, The DE7: Hors W 4C **16**
Crescent, The DE72: Breas 4G **41**
Crescent, The DE72: Ris 6H **33**
Crescent, The DE73: Mel 4D **52**
Cressbrook Way DE21: Oak 4F **25**
Cressida Ct. DE73: Chell 3F **47**
Crest, The DE22: Darl A 5E **23**
Cresta Gro. DE21: Chad 6D **24**
Crewe St. DE23: Derb 2B **36**
CREWTON 3A **38**
Crewton Way DE24: A'ton 4H **37**
Crich Av. DE23: Litt 1F **35**
Crich Circ. DE23: Litt 1G **35**
Crich La. DE56: Ambe 4C **10**
Crich La. DE56: Belp 4C **10**
Crich Vw. Dr. DE56: Heag 1G **11**
Cricketers Ct. DE23: Litt 3H **35**
Cricklewood Rd. DE22: Mack 3F **27**
Cringle M. DE21: Oak 5C **24**
Croft, The DE23: Litt 3H **35**
Croft, The DE56: Bar 2E **15**
Croft, The DE56: Heag 2B **10**
Croft, The DE7: Mor 3G **21**
Croft, The DE72: Dray 5E **41**
Croft, The DE73: Mel 4C **52**
Croft Cl. DE21: Spon 3F **31**
Croft Cl. DE72: Ockb 5A **32**
Croft End DE21: Lit E 5A **20**
Crofters Ct. DE21: Oak 5C **24**
Cft. La. DE21: Bread 4A **24**
Cromarty Cl. DE24: Sinf 1A **46**
Cromer Cl. DE3: Mick 2A **34**
Cromford Dr. DE3: Mick 5C **26**
Cromford Rd. DE21: Chad 1H **29**
Cromford Rd. DE5: Rip 5D **8**
Crompton St. DE1: Derb 5B **4** (5B **28**)
Cromwell Av. DE65: Find 3B **44**
Cromwell Rd. DE23: Derb 1B **36**
Cropton Cl. DE24: A'ton 5C **38**
Crosby St. DE22: Derb 5H **27**
Cross Cl. DE23: Litt 3G **35**
Cross Cl. Wlk. DE23: Litt 3G **35**
Crossdale Gro. DE21: Oak 4G **25**
CROSS HILL 3H **13**
Crosshill DE5: Cod 3H **13**
Cross La. DE5: Cod 2H **13**
Crossley St. DE5: Rip 6D **8**
Cross Side DE6: Clif 5A **6**
Cross St. DE22: Derb 3H **27**
Crownland Dr. DE73: Chell 3A **48**
Crown M. DE22: Derb 6A **28**
Crown St. DE22: Derb 6A **28**
Crown St. DE56: Duff 1E **19**
Crown Ter. DE56: Belp 5B **10**
Crown Wlk. DE1: Derb 4D **4** (4C **28**)
Crown Way DE73: Chell 5H **47**
Crowshaw St. DE24: Derb 3D **36**
Croydon Wlk. DE22: Mack 3D **26**
Crystal Cl. DE3: Mick 5B **26**
Cubley Wlk. DE23: Litt 6G **35**
Cuckmere Cl. DE22: Alles 2H **23**
Cullen Av. DE6: Ash 3D **6**
Cullen Way DE24: Sinf 3A **46**
Culworth Cl. DE56: Belp 5F **11**
Culworth Ct. DE21: Oak 5F **25**
Cumberhills Grange DE56: Duff 3D **18**
Cumberhills Rd. DE56: Duff 4C **18**
Cumberland Av. DE21: Chad 3G **29**

58 A-Z Derby

Ecclesbourne Av. – Gladstone Rd.

Ecclesbourne Av. DE56: Duff 2F 19
Ecclesbourne Cl. DE56: Duff 2E 19
Ecclesbourne Mdws. DE56: Duff 1D 18
Edale Av. DE23: Derb 1A 36
Edale Av. DE24: A'ton 4B 38
Edale Av. DE3: Mick 1B 34
Edale Cl. DE22: Alles 6D 22
Edale Dr. DE21: Spon 6F 31
Edale Way DE56: Belp 4B 10
Eden Rd. DE21: Chad 5A 30
Edensor Dr. DE56: Belp 3E 11
Edensor Sq. DE22: Derb 6A 4 (5A 28)
Eden St. DE24: A'ton 3A 38
Edgbaston Ct. DE23: Litt 3G 35
Edge Hill DE73: Chell 2H 47
Edgelaw Ct. DE24: Sinf 2H 45
Edgware Rd. DE22: Mack 3D 26
Edinburgh Cres. DE24: Allen 1G 47
Edith Wood Cl. DE24: A'ton 6B 38
Edmund Rd. DE21: Spon 6F 31
Edmunds Sq. DE3: Mick 4A 34
Ednaston Av. DE23: Litt 6H 35
Edward Av. DE21: Chad 4A 30
Edward Cres. DE56: Kil 3A 16
Edward St. DE1: Derb 1B 4 (3C 28)
Edward St. DE56: Belp 4C 10
Edwinstowe Rd. DE21: Oak 6E 25
Eggesford Rd. DE24: Sten F 3H 45
Egginton Rd. DE65: Etwa 4B 42
(not continuous)
Egmanton Cl. DE21: Oak 6F 25
Egreaves Av. DE75: Losc 5H 13
Eland Cl. DE21: Spon 3G 31
Eldon Ho. DE1: Derb 6C 4 (5C 28)
(off Rosengrave St.)
Eley Wlk. DE1: Derb 6B 4 (5B 28)
Elgin Av. DE23: Litt 3E 35
Eliot Rd. DE23: Litt 3F 35
Elizabeth Cl. DE21: Chad 4B 30
Elkstone Cl. DE21: Oak 5F 25
Ellastone Gdns. DE24: A'ton 4B 38
Ellendale Rd. DE21: Chad 2B 30
Ellesmere Av. DE24: Derb 1F 37
Ellison Av. DE72: Ast T 6G 49
Elm Av. DE56: Belp 1D 14
Elm Gro. DE21: Chad 4B 30
Elm Gro. DE22: Alles 2D 22
Elm Pk. Ct. DE1: Derb 1A 4 (2B 28)
THE ELMS 1D 12
Elms Av. DE23: Litt 1F 35
Elms Av. DE5: Rip 1D 12
Elms Dr. DE23: Litt 2F 35
Elms Farm Way DE23: Litt 3E 35
Elms Gdn. DE23: Litt 2F 35
Elms Gro. DE65: Etwa 2C 42
Elms St. DE1: Derb 2B 28
Elm St. DE72: Borr 1H 39
Elm Tree Av. DE56: Kil 4A 16
Elmtree Av. DE24: Derb 4D 36
Elmwood Dr. DE21: Bread 5A 24
Elsecar Cl. DE56: Belp 4F 11
Elton Rd. DE24: Derb 4D 36
ELVASTON 5G 39
Elvaston Castle Cvn. Pk. DE72: Elv 4G 39
Elvaston Castle Country Pk. 4E 39
Elvaston La. DE24: A'ton 4B 38
Elvaston St. DE72: Dray 4F 41
Embankment Cl. DE22: Mack 2D 26
Emerald Cl. DE21: Oak 5D 24
Emerson Sq. DE23: Derb 5B 36
Emmas-Williams Ct. DE5: Rip 6D 8
Empress Ct. DE23: Derb 1B 36
Empress Rd. DE23: Derb 6B 28
Endsleigh Gdns. DE22: Mack 3D 26
Enfield Rd. DE22: Mack 3F 27
England Ind. Est. DE1: Derb 4H 27
Ennerdale Wlk. DE21: Chad 5B 24
Ennis Cl. DE21: Chad 2C 30
Enoch Stone Dr. DE21: Chad 5B 30
Enterprise Way DE21: Derb 1F 5 (2D 28)
Epping Cl. DE22: Mack 3C 26
Epworth Dr. DE24: A'ton 1A 48
Eskdale Wlk. DE24: A'ton 5D 38
(off Keldholme La.)
Essex St. DE21: Chad 3F 29
Eton St. DE24: Derb 2G 37
Etruria Gdns. DE1: Derb 2C 28
Etta's Way DE65: Etwa 1B 42
Ettrick Dr. DE24: Sinf 3A 46
ETWALL 1B 42
Etwall By-Pass DE65: Etwa 1A 42
Etwall Leisure Cen. 1B 42
Etwall Rd. DE65: Egg 5B 42
Etwall Rd. DE65: Will 5G 43
Etwall St. DE22: Derb 4H 27
Euston Dr. DE1: Derb 2D 28
Evans Av. DE22: Alles 2G 23
Evanston Gdns. DE21: Chad 3B 30
Evelyn Cl. DE72: Borr 2H 39
Evelyn Gro. DE21: Chad 4A 30
Evergreen Cl. DE21: Oak 5E 25
Evesham Cl. DE21: Chad 6C 24
Excelsior Av. DE24: A'ton 5H 37
Exchange St. DE1: Derb 4D 4 (4C 28)
Exeter Ho. DE1: Derb 3E 5 (4D 28)
Exeter Pl. DE1: Derb 3E 5 (4D 28)
Exeter St. DE1: Derb 2E 5 (3D 28)
Eyam Wlk. DE56: Belp 4C 10
Eyes Ct. DE56: Duff 2E 19
(off Town St.)
Eyrie, The DE24: Sinf 3A 46

F

Fairbourne Dr. DE3: Mick 5B 26
Fairdene Ct. DE23: Derb 1B 36
Faires Cl. DE72: Borr 2B 40
Faire St. DE22: Derb 6A 28
Fairfax Rd. DE23: Derb 1B 36
Fairfield Av. DE72: Borr 6A 32
Fairfield Rd. DE23: Derb 1A 36
Fairfield Rd. DE7: Hors W 4C 16
Fairford Gdns. DE23: Litt 5E 35
Fairisle Cl. DE21: Oak 4G 25
Fairlawns DE56: Duff 2D 18
Fairview Cl. DE23: Litt 3E 35
Fairview Cl. DE56: Kil 4B 16
Fairview Grange DE56: Kil 4B 16
Fairway Cl. DE22: Alles 5D 22
Fairway Cres. DE22: Alles 5D 22
Fairways, The DE6: Clif 6A 6
Fairwood Dr. DE24: A'ton 5D 38
Falconside Dr. DE21: Spon 1F 39
Falcons Ri. DE56: Belp 4E 11
Falcon Way DE24: Sinf 3A 46
Falkirk Av. DE5: Rip 3E 9
Fallow Rd. DE21: Spon 3F 31
Falmouth Rd. DE24: A'ton 6C 38
Falstaff Ct. DE73: Chell 3G 47
Far Cft. DE72: Breas 3H 41
Far La. DE72: Ockb 4B 32
Far Laund DE56: Belp 4D 10
FAR LAUND 3E 11
Farley Rd. DE23: Derb 1H 35
Farm Cl. DE5: Pent 1B 8
Farm Cl. DE56: Belp 5E 11
Farm Cl. DE56: Kil 3A 16
Farm Dr. DE24: A'ton 6A 38
Farmhouse M. DE65: Find 3B 44
Farmhouse Rd. DE24: Sinf 3A 46
Farmlands La. DE23: Litt 5F 35
Farm St. DE22: Derb 6A 4 (5B 28)
Farnborough Gdns. DE22: Alles 3H 23
Farncombe La. DE21: Oak 4D 24
Farndale Ct. DE24: A'ton 5C 38
Farneworth Rd. DE3: Mick 1B 34
Farnham Cl. DE3: Mick 2A 34
Farningham Cl. DE21: Spon 4F 31
Farnway DE22: Darl A 5E 23
Farrier Gdns. DE23: Litt 4E 35
Farringdon Cl. DE22: Mack 3D 26
Faversham Cl. DE24: A'ton 6H 37
Fearn Av. DE5: Rip 6E 9
Fellow Lands Way DE73: Chell 2A 48
Fellside DE21: Spon 3F 31
Fellside DE56: Belp 5C 10
Fenchurch Wlk. DE22: Mack 3F 27
Fenton Rd. DE3: Mick 1A 34
Fenwick St. DE24: Derb 4F 37
Ferncroft Wlk. DE73: Chell 3H 47
Fernhill Ct. DE73: Chell 2A 48
Fernilee Gdns. DE21: Chad 6D 24
Fernwood Cl. DE23: Litt 3G 35
Ferrers Cres. DE56: Duff 2D 18
Ferrers Way DE22: Darl A 5E 23
Ferrers Way DE5: Rip 4C 8
Festival Av. DE72: Breas 4G 41
Field Cl. DE72: Borr 6H 31
Field Ct. DE56: Kil 4A 16
Field Cres. DE24: A'ton 6A 38
Field Dr. DE24: A'ton 6A 38
Field Dr. DE7: Smal 3H 17
Fieldfare Ct. DE23: Litt 5E 35
Fieldgate Dr. DE21: Oak 5D 24
Field Head Way DE21: Oak 4F 25
Field La. DE21: Chad 2H 29
Field La. DE24: A'ton 5B 38
Field La. DE56: Belp 5B 10
Field Ri. DE23: Litt 4G 35
Field Row DE56: Belp 5B 10
Field St. DE5: Cod 2H 13
Fieldsway Dr. DE21: Chad 5B 24
Field Ter. DE5: Rip 6D 8
Field Vw. Cl. DE24: A'ton 1B 48
Fife St. DE24: A'ton 3G 37
Filbert Wlk. DE73: Chell 5A 48
Filey Wlk. DE21: Chad 6B 24
Fincham Cl. DE21: Chad 6B 24
Finch Cres. DE3: Mick 3A 34
Finchley Av. DE22: Mack 3D 26
FINDERN 4B 44
Findern Cl. DE22: Alles 6D 22
Findern Cl. DE56: Belp 3D 10
Findern La. DE65: Burn 1G 43
Findern St. DE22: Derb 4H 27
Finmere Cl. DE23: Litt 3E 35
Finningley Dr. DE22: Darl A 5E 23
Finsbury Av. DE22: Mack 3F 27
Finsley Wlk. DE23: Derb 4A 36
Firs, The DE6: Ash 3D 6
Firs Av. DE5: Rip 6D 8
Firs Cres. DE22: Alles 3E 23
Firtree Gro. DE21: Oak 5F 25
Fisher La. DE56: Duff 1E 19
Fisher St. DE24: Allen 5G 37
Fiskerton Way DE21: Oak 1B 30
Fitness First Derby 1E 5 (3D 28)
Fitzwilliam Cl. DE3: Mick 6D 26
Five Lamps DE1: Derb 1B 4 (2B 28)
Five Lamps Ct. DE1: Derb 1A 4 (3B 28)
Flamstead Av. DE75: Losc 5H 13
Flamstead La. DE5: Denb 2D 16
Flamstead St. DE24: Allen 5G 37
Flat, The DE56: Kil 3H 15
FLAXHOLME 4F 19
Flaxholme Av. DE56: Duff 4F 19
Fleet, The DE56: Belp 1B 14
Fleet Cres. DE56: Belp 6B 10
Fleet Pk. DE56: Belp 6C 10
Fleet St. DE23: Derb 1C 36
Fletcher's Row DE5: Rip 5F 9
Fletcher St. DE5: Rip 5E 9
Flint St. DE24: Allen 5F 37
Flood St. DE72: Ockb 5A 32
Florence Ct. DE1: Derb 6G 5 (5E 29)
Folkestone Dr. DE24: A'ton 6A 38
Folly Rd. DE22: Darl A 6H 23
Ford Av. DE75: Losc 5H 13
Ford Cl. DE5: Rip 1C 12
Ford La. DE21: Lit E 2A 24
Ford La. DE22: Alles 2G 23
(not continuous)
Ford St. DE1: Derb 3B 4 (4B 28)
Ford St. DE56: Belp 5B 10
Fordwells Cl. DE23: Litt 3E 35
Fordyce Cl. DE73: Chell 4G 47
Foremark Av. DE23: Derb 3A 36
Forest Cl. DE56: Belp 4D 10
Forester's Leisure Pk. 4C 36
Foresters Rd. DE5: Rip 5C 8
Forester St. DE1: Derb 5C 4 (5C 28)
Forester St. W. DE1: Derb 5B 4 (5B 28)
Forester's Way DE23: Derb 4C 36
Forman St. DE1: Derb 4B 4 (4B 28)
Forshaw Cl. DE6: Ash 4D 6
Forty Foot La. DE73: Wils 6G 53
Forty Horse Cl. DE5: Rip 6G 9
Forum Cl. DE24: A'ton 6D 38
Fosse Cl. DE72: Borr 2A 40
Foundry La. DE56: Mil 4B 14
Fountains Cl. DE22: Alles 3G 23
Fowler Av. DE21: Spon 5D 30
Fowler St. DE1: Derb 4A 28
Fowler St. DE72: Dray 4F 41
Foxbrook Cl. DE23: Litt 3E 35
Fox Cl. DE24: Sten F 2H 45
Foxdell Way DE73: Chell 3A 48
Foxes Wlk. DE22: Alles 3E 23
Foxfields Dr. DE21: Oak 5C 24
Foxglove Dr. DE21: Oak 4D 24
Foxlands Av. DE22: Darl A 5F 23
Foxley Ct. DE21: Oak 5F 25
Fox St. DE1: Derb 1D 4 (3C 28)
Foyle Av. DE21: Chad 5A 30
Frampton Gdns. DE23: Litt 5D 34
Franchise Ct. DE22: Derb 5A 28
Franchise St. DE22: Derb 5A 28
Francis St. DE21: Chad 2H 5 (3F 29)
Franklyn Dr. DE24: A'ton 5A 38
Frazer Cl. DE21: Spon 3E 31
Frederick Av. DE24: A'ton 5H 37
Frederick St. DE22: Derb 3H 27
Freehold St. DE22: Derb 5A 28
Freeman Av. DE23: Derb 5A 36
Freesia Cl. DE3: Mick 2C 34
Fremantle Rd. DE3: Mick 6C 26
French La. DE21: Hors 6H 15
French St. DE23: Derb 1A 36
Fresco Dr. DE23: Litt 4D 34
Freshwater Ho. DE24: A'ton 4C 38
(off Durley Cl.)
Friar Ga. DE1: Derb 2A 4 (4B 28)
Friar Ga. Ct. DE1: Derb 3A 4 (4B 28)
Friargate M. DE1: Derb 4B 4 (4B 28)
Friars Cl. DE22: Darl A 5F 23
Friary Av. DE24: Allen 6G 37
Friary St. DE1: Derb 4B 4 (4B 28)
Fritchley Cl. DE21: Chad 6E 25
Frizams La. DE65: Twy 6D 44
Frizams La. DE73: Twy 6D 44
Froggatt Cl. DE22: Alles 2G 23
Fulbrook Rd. DE23: Litt 3E 35
Fulham Rd. DE22: Mack 4E 27
Fullers Cl. DE56: Mil 4B 14
Full St. DE1: Derb 2C 4 (3C 28)
Fulmar Cl. DE3: Mick 6E 27
Furrows Cl. DE21: Oak 4G 25

G

Gable Ct. DE3: Mick 3C 34
Gables, The 1B 30
Gainsborough Cl. DE21: Oak 6F 25
Gairloch Cl. DE24: Sten F 3H 45
Gala Bingo Derby, Forester's Way 4C 36
Gala Bingo Derby, Liversage St. 5F 5 (5D 28)
Gala Dr. DE24: A'ton 4H 37
Galway Av. DE21: Chad 5B 30
Garden Lodge Cl. DE23: Derb 1H 35
Gardens, The DE5: Rip 2D 12
Garden St. DE1: Derb 1B 4 (2B 28)
Garfield Av. DE72: Dray 4E 41
Garfield Cl. DE23: Litt 5G 35
Garrick St. DE24: A'ton 4A 38
Garry Cl. DE24: Sten F 3H 45
Garsdale Ct. DE24: A'ton 5D 38
Garth Cres. DE24: A'ton 5B 38
Garthorpe Ct. DE21: Oak 5D 24
Gary Cl. DE23: Litt 6H 35
Gascoigne Dr. DE21: Spon 5D 30
Gaskell Av. DE23: Derb 4A 36
Gatcombe Cl. DE21: Oak 5F 25
Gate Brook Cl. DE5: Cod 6H 9
Gayton Av. DE23: Litt 5H 35
Gayton Thorpe Cl. DE23: Litt 4D 34
Gema Cl. DE22: Alles 3G 23
George Cres. DE55: Ridd 1H 9
George Dutton Bus. Pk. DE6: Ash 4F 7
George St. DE1: Derb 3B 4 (4B 28)
George St. DE56: Belp 5B 10
George St. DE6: Ash 4C 6
George St. DE73: Mel 5C 52
George Yd. DE1: Derb 3C 4 (4C 28)
Gerard Cl. DE21: Spon 3F 31
Gerard Ct. DE1: Derb 5B 4 (5B 28)
Gerard Gro. DE65: Etwa 1C 42
Gerard St. DE1: Derb 6B 4 (5B 28)
Gerard St. Nth. DE1: Derb 5B 4 (5B 28)
Gertrude Rd. DE21: Chad 1H 29
Gertrude Rd. DE72: Dray 4E 41
Ghyll Cl. DE24: A'ton 2A 38
Gibfield La. DE56: Belp 1B 14
Gilbert Cl. DE21: Spon 5D 30
Gilbert Cres. DE56: Duff 3E 19
Gilbert St. DE24: A'ton 6B 38
(not continuous)
Gilderdale Way DE21: Oak 4F 25
Gillamoor Ct. DE24: A'ton 5C 38
Gill Ct. DE56: Belp 6B 10
Gilliver Gdns. DE72: Dray 4E 41
Girton Way DE3: Mick 6D 26
Gisborne Cl. DE3: Mick 6C 26
Gisborne Cres. DE22: Alles 3F 23
Gisborne Grn. DE1: Derb 1A 4 (3A 28)
Gladstone Cl. DE73: Chell 2H 47
Gladstone Rd. DE21: Spon 4E 31

60 A-Z Derby

Gladstone St. – Hermitage Av.

Gladstone St. DE23: Derb 2A **36**
Glaisdale Nook DE24: A'ton 5D **38**
(not continuous)
Glamis Cl. DE21: Oak 5F **25**
Glasshouse Hill DE5: Cod 6H **9**
Glastonbury Rd. DE24: A'ton 4C **38**
Gleadsmoss La. DE21: Oak 6E **25**
Glebe Av. DE5: Rip 5C **8**
Glebe Av. DE7: Smal 5F **17**
Glebe Ri. DE23: Litt 2G **35**
Glen Av. DE56: Hol 4E **15**
Glencroft Dr. DE24: Sten F 2H **45**
Glendale Dr. DE21: Spon 4F **31**
Glendevon Way DE73: Chell 3G **47**
Glendon Rd. DE24: Sten F 2H **45**
Gleneagles Cl. DE3: Mick 1D **34**
Glenfield Cres. DE3: Mick 1A **34**
Glengarry Way DE24: Sinf 1A **46**
Glenmore Dr. DE24: Sten F 1H **45**
Glenmoy Cl. DE23: Derb 4H **35**
Glenn Way DE72: Shard 4B **50**
Glenorchy Ct. DE21: Oak 4F **25**
Glen Pk. Cl. DE73: Chell 5H **47**
Glenshee Gdns. DE73: Chell 3G **47**
Glen Vw. DE56: Belp 1B **14**
Glen Vine DE5: Rip 6G **9**
Glenwood Rd. DE73: Chell 5A **48**
(not continuous)
Glossop St. DE24: Derb 4D **36**
Gloster St. DE24: Derb 1G **37**
Goathland Rd. DE24: Sten F 3H **45**
Goldcrest Dr. DE21: Spon 3F **31**
Golden Valley DE7: Hors W 4B **16**
Golden Valley Country Pk. 3H **9**
Golden Valley Light Railway Butterley Pk. Station 3G **9**
Golden Valley Light Railway Newlands Inn Station 4H **9**
Golders Grn. Wlk. DE22: Mack 3E **27**
Gold La. DE22: Mack 1C **26**
Goldstone Ct. DE21: Spon 5E **31**
Golf Cl. DE23: Litt 2E **35**
Golf La. DE56: Duff 6A **14**
Goodale St. DE23: Derb 2C **36**
Good Hope Ct. DE24: Derb 1G **37**
Goodricke Ct. DE3: Mick 6D **26**
Goodrington Rd. DE21: Oak 4G **25**
Goodsmoor Rd. DE23: Litt 6H **35**
Goodsmoor Rd. DE24: Sinf 6A **36**
Goodsmoor Rd. Ind. Est. DE24: Sinf 6A **36**
Goods Rd. DE56: Belp 1B **14**
Goods Rd. Ind. Est. DE56: Belp 1B **14**
Goods Yd. DE56: Belp 2B **14**
Goodwood Dr. DE24: A'ton 5C **38**
Goose La. DE5: Cod 1H **13**
Gordon Rd. DE23: Derb 6B **28**
Gordon Rd. DE72: Borr 2H **39**
Gorse Cl. DE23: Litt 5F **35**
Gorsehill Gro. DE23: Litt 4E **35**
Gorsey Cl. DE56: Belp 3A **10**
Gorsty Leys DE65: Find 4B **44**
Gosforth Rd. DE24: Derb 4G **37**
Gower St. DE1: Derb 5C **4** (5C **28**)
Grafham Cl. DE73: Chell 3A **48**
Grafton St. DE23: Derb 1A **36**
Grammer St. DE5: Denb 5G **13**
Grampian Way DE24: Sten F 2H **45**
Grandstand Rd. DE21: Chad 1H **5** (3E **29**)
Grange, The DE7: Smal 3H **17**
Grange Av. DE23: Derb 4A **36**
Grange Av. DE72: Breas 3H **41**
Grange Cl. DE73: Mel 4D **52**
Grange Ga. DE22: Derb 6B **28**
Grangeover Way DE22: Derb 5G **27**
Grange Rd. DE24: A'ton 6B **38**
Grange St. DE23: Derb 1D **36**
(not continuous)
Grangewood Dr. DE56: Mil 4C **14**
Grant Av. DE21: Chad 4B **30**
Grantham Av. DE21: Chad 6B **24**
Granville Cl. DE56: Duff 2E **19**
Granville St. DE1: Derb 4A **28**
Grasmere Av. DE21: Spon 3E **31**
Grasmere Cres. DE24: Sinf 1A **46**
Grassthorpe Cl. DE21: Oak 6F **25**
Grassy La. DE23: Litt 4G **35**
Gravel Pit La. DE21: Spon 4E **31**
Grayling St. DE23: Derb 1D **36**
Gt. Northern Ct. DE1: Derb 4A **4** (4A **28**)
Gt. Northern Rd. DE1: Derb 4A **28**
Greatorex Av. DE24: Allen 6G **37**
Gt. Willow Ct. DE22: Derb 5G **27**
Greaves St. DE5: Rip 5E **9**
Green, The DE21: Hors 5H **15**
Green, The DE22: Alles 6D **22**
Green, The DE3: Mick 2B **34**
Green, The DE56: Belp 4C **10**
(off Acorn Dr.)
Green, The DE65: Find 4B **44**
Green, The DE72: Ast T 5H **49**
Green, The DE72: Breas 3H **41**
Green, The DE72: Dray 4E **41**
Greenacre, The DE6: Clif 5A **6**
Greenacres DE23: Litt 3F **35**
Green Av. DE73: Chell 4A **48**
Grn. Bank DE21: Spon 5D **30**
Greenburn Cl. DE23: Litt 5G **35**
Greenfields Av. DE23: Litt 4F **35**
Greenfinch Cl. DE21: Spon 3F **31**
Greenhill Av. DE5: Rip 1E **13**
Greenhill Ind. Est. DE55: Ridd 1H **9**
GREENHILLOCKS 2D **12**
Greenland Av. DE22: Mack 4F **27**
Green La. DE1: Derb 5C **4** (4C **28**)
Green La. DE24: A'ton 3B **38**
Green La. DE56: Belp 5B **10**
Green La. DE6: Ash 4A **6**
Green La. DE65: Burn 1F **43**
Green La. DE72: Ockb 4A **32**
Grn. Leas DE72: Ast T 5G **49**
Greenmount Cl. DE23: Litt 5E **35**
Green Pk. DE22: Mack 3E **27**
Green Rd., The DE6: Ash 1D **6**
Greenside Ct. DE3: Mick 1A **34**
Greenside Vw. DE7: Smal 5F **17**
Greenville Cft. DE73: Chell 4G **47**
Greenway DE6: Ash 1D **6**
Greenway DE65: Find 3B **44**
Greenway, The DE72: Elv 6D **38**
Greenway Cl. DE72: Borr 6H **31**
Greenway Dr. DE23: Litt 2E **35**
GREENWICH 5E **9**
Greenwich Dr. Nth. DE22: Mack 3F **27**
Greenwich Dr. Sth. DE22: Mack 4E **27**
Greenwood Av. DE21: Chad 1H **29**
Greenwood Ct. DE1: Derb 2D **4** (3C **28**)
Gregory Av. DE72: Breas 3G **41**
Gregorys Way DE56: Belp 4E **11**
Gregory Wlk. DE23: Litt 4C **34**
Grendon Cl. DE56: Belp 3D **10**
Grenfell Av. DE23: Derb 5A **36**
Grenvoir Dr. DE5: Rip 6G **9**
Gresham Rd. DE24: Derb 3E **37**
Greyfriars Pl. DE3: Mick 6D **26**
Grey St. DE1: Derb 6B **4** (5B **28**)
Griffin Cl. DE24: A'ton 4H **37**
Grimshaw Av. DE24: A'ton 4B **38**
Grindlow Rd. DE21: Chad 1A **30**
Groombridge Cres. DE23: Litt 5E **35**
Groome Av. DE75: Losc 5H **13**
Grosvenor Dr. DE23: Litt 5E **35**
Grosvenor Rd. DE5: Rip 6D **8**
Grosvenor St. DE24: Derb 2E **37**
(not continuous)
Grove, The DE3: Mick 1C **34**
Grove, The DE5: Rip 6D **8**
Grovebury Dr. DE23: Litt 6G **35**
Grove Cl. DE72: Thul 1F **49**
Grove Ct. DE5: Rip 1F **13**
Grove Ct. DE72: Thul 1F **49**
Grove Ho. DE23: Derb 6C **28**
Grove Pk. DE65: Etwa 3B **42**
Groves Nook DE73: Chell 4G **47**
Grove St. DE23: Derb 6C **28**
Guildhall Theatre 3D **4** (4C **28**)
Gurney Av. DE23: Derb 5H **35**
Gypsy La. DE72: Dray 3C **40**

H

Haddon Cl. DE22: Alles 4D **22**
Haddon Ct. DE6: Ash 4E **7**
Haddon Dr. DE21: Lit E 3A **20**
Haddon Dr. DE21: Spon 5F **31**
Haddon Dr. DE22: Alles 4D **22**
Haddon Dr. DE3: Mick 6C **26**
Haddon St. DE23: Derb 2A **36**
Haig St. DE24: A'ton 3H **37**
Hailsham Cl. DE3: Mick 6B **26**
Hains Cl. DE24: Sinf 1B **46**
Halcyon DE22: Derb 3A **28**
(off Ashbourne Rd.)
Halifax Cl. DE21: Chad 6A **24**
Hall Dyke DE21: Spon 4D **30**
Hall Farm Rd. DE56: Duff 3E **19**
Hall Farm Way DE7: Smal 4F **17**
Hallgate Cl. DE21: Oak 4G **25**
Hall La. DE6: Ash 2D **6**
Hall Leys La. DE73: King N 2F **53**
Hall Pk. Cl. DE23: Litt 2F **35**
Hall Ri. DE6: Ash 1E **7**
Hall Rd. DE5: Denb 4D **12**
Hall St. DE24: A'ton 4A **38**
Halstock Dr. DE24: A'ton 3C **38**
Hambledon Dr. DE24: Sten F 3H **45**
Hambleton Cl. DE6: Ash 4D **6**
Hamblin Cres. DE24: Sinf 1B **46**
Hamilton Cl. DE3: Mick 6D **26**
Hamilton Rd. DE21: Spon 3F **31**
Hamilton Rd. DE23: Derb 1B **36**
Hamlet Ct. DE73: Chell 4G **47**
Hammersmith DE5: Rip 4D **8**
HAMMERSMITH 3D **8**
Hammersmith Station Midland Railway 3D **8**
Hampden St. DE23: Derb 3C **36**
Hampshire Rd. DE21: Chad 1E **29**
Hampstead Dr. DE22: Mack 3E **27**
Hampton Cl. DE21: Spon 4F **31**
Hanbury Rd. DE21: Chad 3G **29**
Handel M. DE6: Ash 4E **7**
Handel St. DE24: Derb 3E **37**
Handford Ct. DE1: Derb 4A **28**
Handford St. DE22: Derb 4H **27**
Handyside Ct. DE24: A'ton 4H **37**
Handyside St. DE1: Derb 1C **4** (3C **28**)
Hanger Bank DE72: Ast T 5H **49**
HANGINGBRIDGE 4A **6**
Hanover Sq. DE22: Mack 3E **27**
Hansard Ga. DE21: Derb 3G **5** (4E **29**)
Hanslynn DE72: Thul 1F **49**
Hanwell Way DE22: Mack 3F **27**
Harboro Cl. DE6: Ash 4C **6**
Harcourt St. DE1: Derb 6B **4** (5B **28**)
Hardacre Cl. DE73: Mel 4C **52**
Hardhurst Rd. DE24: A'ton 6B **38**
Hardwick Av. DE22: Alles 4D **22**
Hardwick Cl. DE5: Rip 4C **8**
Hardwick Dr. DE3: Mick 1C **34**
Hardwick St. DE24: Derb 3E **37**
Hardy Cres. DE5: Cod 1H **13**
Harebell Cl. DE21: Oak 4E **25**
Harepit Cl. DE24: A'ton 6A **38**
Harewood Cl. DE56: Belp 4F **11**
Harewood Rd. DE22: Alles 4D **22**
Hargrave Av. DE72: Ockb 4A **32**
Hargreaves Cl. DE23: Litt 5E **35**
Harlech Cl. DE21: Spon 4G **31**
Harlesden Av. DE22: Mack 2E **27**
Harlow Cl. DE24: A'ton 1H **47**
Harold Ct. DE23: Derb 1D **36**
Harpswell Cl. DE22: Darl A 5E **23**
Harpur Av. DE23: Litt 4F **35**
Harrier Rd. DE56: Belp 4E **11**
Harrier Way DE24: Sinf 2A **46**
Harriet St. DE23: Derb 6C **28**
Harriet Tubman Ho. DE23: Derb 2B **36**
Harringay Gdns. DE22: Mack 3G **27**
Harrington Av. DE72: Borr 1A **40**
Harrington Rd. DE23: Litt 2G **35**
Harrington St. DE23: Derb 3C **36**
Harrington St. DE24: Allen 5G **37**
Harrington St. DE72: Dray 4F **41**
Harris Av. DE5: Rip 5C **8**
Harris Cl. DE5: Rip 6C **8**
Harrison St. DE22: Derb 6A **28**
Harrogate Cres. DE21: Chad 6B **24**
Harrow St. DE24: Derb 2G **37**
Hartington M. DE23: Derb 6C **28**
(off Hartington St.)
Hartington St. DE23: Derb 6C **28**
Hartington Way DE3: Mick 2B **34**
Hartland Dr. DE23: Derb 5A **36**
Hartshay Hill DE5: Low H 4B **8**
Hartshay Hill DE5: Rip 4C **8**
Hartshorne Rd. DE23: Litt 5G **35**
Harvester Cl. DE5: Rip 5C **8**
Harvest Way DE21: Oak 4G **25**
Harvey Rd. DE24: Allen 5G **37**
Harvey Rd. DE24: A'ton 5G **37**
Hasgill Cl. DE21: Oak 4G **25**
Haskeys Cl. DE22: Alles 5C **22**
Haslam Pl. DE56: Belp 2E **15**
Haslam's La. DE22: Darl A 6H **23**
Haslemere Ct. DE23: Derb 1D **36**
Hassop Rd. DE21: Chad 1A **30**
Hastings St. DE23: Derb 2C **36**
(not continuous)
Hatchmere Cl. DE21: Oak 6E **25**
Hatfield Rd. DE24: A'ton 6H **37**
Hathern Cl. DE23: Derb 6A **36**
Hathersage Av. DE23: Derb 3A **36**
Hattons Ct. DE73: Mel 5C **52**
Havelock Rd. DE23: Derb 3B **36**
Havelock St. DE5: Rip 5E **9**
Havenbaulk Av. DE23: Litt 4C **34**
Haven Baulk La. DE23: Litt 4C **34**
Haven Ct. DE24: A'ton 5D **38**
Havenwood Gro. DE23: Litt 6G **35**
Hawke St. DE22: Derb 4G **27**
Hawksdale Cl. DE73: Chell 3A **48**
Hawkshead Av. DE21: Chad 6B **24**
Hawthorn Av. DE5: Rip 1D **12**
Hawthorn Cl. DE6: Ash 4E **7**
Hawthorn Ct. DE1: Derb 1A **4** (2B **28**)
Hawthorn Cres. DE65: Find 3B **44**
Hawthorne Av. DE24: A'ton 4A **38**
Hawthorne Av. DE72: Borr 6H **31**
Hawthorne Cl. DE56: Kil 1H **15**
Hawthorns, The DE21: Lit E 5B **20**
Hawthorns, The DE56: Belp 4F **11**
Hawthorn St. DE24: Derb 3E **37**
Hawtrey Gdns. DE24: A'ton 5A **38**
Haycroft Ct. DE23: Litt 4E **35**
Haydn Rd. DE21: Chad 1H **29**
Haydock Pk. Rd. DE24: Derb 3G **37**
Hayes, The DE65: Find 4A **44**
Hayes Av. DE23: Derb 3H **35**
Hayes Av. DE72: Breas 4F **41**
Hayes Cres. DE55: Swan 1F **9**
Hayes La. DE55: Swan 1F **9**
Hayfield Cl. DE56: Belp 4D **10**
Hayfield Gdns. DE23: Litt 5F **35**
Hayford Pl. DE22: Derb 5H **27**
Hayley Cft. DE56: Duff 4F **19**
Haymarket DE1: Derb 4C **4** (4C **28**)
(off Strand)
Haywood Cl. DE24: A'ton 6A **38**
Hazel Av. DE23: Litt 5H **35**
Hazel Cl. DE6: Ash 4E **7**
Hazel Cl. DE65: Find 3C **44**
Hazeldene Cl. DE56: Duff 6A **14**
Hazel Dr. DE21: Spon 3G **31**
Hazel Gro. DE56: Duff 2E **19**
Hazeltree Cl. DE5: Rip 1C **12**
Hazelwood Rd. DE21: Chad 1H **29**
Headingley Ct. DE23: Litt 3G **35**
HEAGE 2B **10**
Heage Rd. DE5: Rip 6B **8**
Heage Rd. Ind. Est. DE5: Rip 6B **8**
Heanor Ho. DE21: Spon 6E **31**
Heanor Rd. DE5: Cod 2H **13**
Heanor Rd. DE5: Denb 6G **13**
Heanor Rd. DE7: Smal 5F **17**
Heath Av. DE23: Litt 2G **35**
Heathcote Cl. DE24: A'ton 6B **38**
Heathcotes Cotts. DE1: Derb 6C **28**
Heath Ct. DE24: Sinf 2A **46**
Heather Cl. DE24: Sten F 3H **45**
Heather Cres. DE23: Litt 5G **35**
Heathermead Cl. DE21: Oak 6D **24**
HEATHERTON 5E **35**
Heath La. DE65: Find 5B **44**
(not continuous)
Heath Rd. DE5: Rip 6D **8**
Hebden Cl. DE23: Litt 5D **34**
Hebrides Cl. DE24: Sinf 2H **45**
Hedgebank Ct. DE21: Oak 4G **25**
Hedgerow Gdns. DE21: Oak 4G **25**
Hedgevale Cl. DE23: Litt 4E **35**
Hedingham Way DE3: Mick 2A **34**
Heigham Cl. DE24: Shel L 2F **47**
Helston Cl. DE24: A'ton 5B **38**
Hemlock Cl. DE21: Oak 4E **25**
Hendon Way DE22: Mack 3F **27**
Henley Grn. DE22: Mack 3D **26**
Henmore Pl. DE6: Ash 2D **6**
Henmore Trad. Est. DE6: Ash 4B **6**
Henry St. DE1: Derb 1B **4** (3B **28**)
(not continuous)
Henry St. DE5: Rip 5D **8**
Herald Gro. DE73: Chell 5G **47**
Hereford Rd. DE21: Chad 1F **29**
Heritage Bus. Cen. DE56: Belp 2B **14**
Heritage Ct. DE56: Belp 6B **10**
Heritage Ga. DE1: Derb 3B **4** (4B **28**)
(off Friary St.)
Hermitage Av. DE55: Ridd 2H **9**

Kingfisher Cl. – Lowes La.

Kingfisher Cl. DE3: Mick....4A 34
Kingfisher Wlk. DE24: Sinf....3A 46
Kingsbury Rd. DE22: Mack....3E 27
Kingsclere Av. DE21: Oak....5F 25
Kings Ct. DE1: Derb....1C 4 (3C 28)
Kings Cft. DE22: Alles....3F 23
Kingsdale Gro. DE73: Chell....5H 47
Kings Dr. DE23: Litt....1F 35
Kingsland Cl. DE21: Oak....5D 24
Kingsley Rd. DE22: Alles....4D 22
Kingsley St. DE24: Sinf....6B 36
Kingsmead Cl. DE1: Derb....1B 4 (3B 28)
King's Mead Ho. DE22: Derb....2B 28
Kingsmead Ind. Est. DE22: Derb....3H 27
Kingsmead Wlk. DE1: Derb....1B 4 (3B 28)
Kingsmuir Rd. DE3: Mick....6A 26
KING'S NEWTON....3D 52
Kings Newton La. DE73: Mel....3C 52
Kingston St. DE1: Derb....2B 28
KINGS TREATMENT CEN.....1F 35
King St. DE1: Derb....1B 4 (3B 28)
King St. DE56: Belp....6B 10
King St. DE56: Duff....1E 19
King St. DE6: Ash....2D 6
Kingsway DE22: Derb....4F 27
Kingsway Cres. DE56: Kil....3A 16
KINGSWAY HOSPITAL....5F 27
Kingsway Ind. Pk. DE22: Derb....4G 27
Kingsway Pk. Cl. DE22: Derb....4F 27
Kingsway Retail Pk. Derby....5G 27
Kingswood Av. DE56: Belp....3E 11
Kingswood Pl. DE23: Litt....2F 35
Kinross Av. DE21: Chad....1E 29
Kintyre Dr. DE24: Sinf....2H 45
Kipling Dr. DE3: Mick....2B 34
Kirk Cl. DE5: Rip....1C 12
Kirkdale Av. DE21: Spon....6F 31
Kirkfield Dr. DE72: Breas....3H 41
Kirkistown Cl. DE24: A'ton....5C 38
Kirkland Way DE24: Sten F....2H 45
Kirk Leys Av. Nth. DE21: Spon....5E 31
Kirkleys Av. Sth. DE21: Spon....5E 31
Kirk's La. DE56: Belp....6D 10
Kirkstead Cl. DE21: Oak....6F 25
Kirk St. DE1: Derb....2C 28
Kitchener Av. DE23: Derb....4B 36
Kiwi Dr. DE24: A'ton....3H 37
Knife & Steel Ct. DE7: Hors W....4C 16
Knightsbridge DE22: Mack....3E 27
Knights Cl. DE24: Sten F....3A 46
Knights Rd. DE73: Chell....5G 47
Kniveton Cl. DE22: Derb....3H 27
Knoll Cl. DE23: Litt....3E 35
Knowl Av. DE56: Belp....3A 10
Knutsford Grn. DE21: Chad....5B 24
Kraft Gdns. DE21: Chad....4B 30
Kyle Gro. DE21: Oak....4F 25
Kynance Cl. DE24: A'ton....6C 38

L

Laburnum Cres. DE22: Alles....2D 22
Laburnum Gro. DE22: Mack....4E 27
Laburnum Way DE65: Etwa....2C 42
Lace Makers Cl. DE72: Borr....2B 40
Ladbroke Gdns. DE22: Mack....3D 26
Ladybank Rd. DE3: Mick....6A 26
Ladybower Rd. DE21: Spon....5F 31
Ladycroft Paddock DE22: Alles....3E 23
Ladygrove Cotts. DE23: Derb....6D 28
Ladygrove Ter. DE24: A'ton....4A 38
....(off Baker St.)
Lady Hole La. DE6: Yeld....6H 7
Lady La. DE5: Denb....2C 16
Lady Lea Rd. DE21: Hors....5A 16
Lady Lea Rd. DE7: Hors W....5B 16
Lady Mantle Cl. DE73: Chell....4H 47
Ladysmith Rd. DE72: Borr....1H 39
Ladywell Ct. DE56: Belp....6C 10
Lady Wells Views DE56: Belp....5C 10
....(off Springwood Gdns.)
Ladywood Av. DE56: Belp....4D 10
Lake Dr. DE23: Derb....3B 36
Lakeside DE6: Ash....2D 6
Lakeside Dr. DE23: Litt....4D 34
Lamb Cres. DE5: Rip....6E 9
Lambe Ct. DE23: Derb....6D 28
Lambley Dr. DE22: Alles....5C 22
Lambourn Ct. DE22: Alles....4G 23
Lambourn Dr. DE22: Alles....3G 23
Lambourne Av. DE6: Ash....4E 7
Lambrook Cl. DE3: Mick....1A 34
Lampad Cl. DE73: Mel....4C 52
Lampeter Cl. DE21: Oak....5F 25
Lanark St. DE21: Chad....2G 29
Lancaster Ri. DE56: Belp....3C 10
Lancaster Wlk. DE21: Spon....3G 31
Lander La. DE56: Belp....5C 10
Landmere DE24: Sinf....2A 46
Lane, The DE5: Rip....5C 8
Langdale Dr. DE21: Chad....6B 24
Langford Rd. DE3: Mick....6B 26
Langley Rd. DE21: Spon....6E 31
Langley St. DE22: Derb....4H 27
Lang Rd. DE24: A'ton....5H 37
Langsett Dr. DE73: Chell....3A 48
Langwith Cl. DE3: Mick....1D 34
Lanscombe Pk. Rd. DE22: Darl A....6E 23
Lansdowne Av. DE24: A'ton....6H 37
Lansing Gdns. DE21: Chad....3B 30
Lantern Gro. DE3: Mick....5B 26
Lapwing Cl. DE24: Sinf....3A 46
Lapwing Cl. DE56: Kil....3A 16
Lara Cft. Way DE1: Derb....6C 4 (5C 28)
Larch Av. DE5: Rip....6D 8
Larch Cl. DE22: Alles....4D 22
Larch Rd. DE56: Kil....4B 16
Larges St. DE1: Derb....3A 4 (4A 28)
Lark Cl. DE23: Litt....5G 35
Lark Hill DE3: Mick....6A 34
Larkhill Cres. DE24: Sinf....1B 46
Larkin Cl. DE24: Sinf....6C 36
Larkspur Ct. DE21: Oak....4E 25
Lashley Gdns. DE21: Oak....5D 24
Lathbury Cl. DE21: Chad....6B 24
Lathkill Av. DE24: A'ton....4C 38
Lathkill Dr. DE5: Mare....3D 12
Lathkill Dr. DE6: Ash....4F 7
Lathkill Rd. DE21: Chad....1H 29
Latimer Cl. DE23: Litt....4C 34
Latimer St. DE24: Derb....5F 37
Latrigg Cl. DE3: Mick....2C 34
Lauder Cl. DE24: Sinf....3A 46
Launceston Rd. DE24: A'ton....6B 38
Laund Av. DE56: Belp....3D 10
Laund Cl. DE56: Belp....3C 10
Laund Farm M. DE56: Belp....3E 11
Laund Hill DE56: Belp....4C 10
Laund Nook DE56: Belp....4C 10
Laurel Av. DE5: Rip....6D 8
Laurel Bank DE23: Derb....3B 36
Laurel Cres. DE7: Smal....6F 17
Laurel Dr. DE72: Ast T....6G 49
Laurie Pl. DE24: Allen....4G 37
Lavender Row DE22: Darl A....6F 23
Laverstoke Ct. DE22: Derb....5A 28
Lavina Ct. DE73: Chell....3G 47
Lawn Av. DE22: Alles....5D 22
Lawn Heads Av. DE23: Litt....1G 35
Lawnlea Cl. DE23: Derb....6A 36
Lawns, The DE72: Ast T....5H 49
Lawnside DE21: Spon....4F 31
Lawnswood Cl. DE23: Litt....3G 35
Lawrence Av. DE21: Chad....2B 30
Lawrence Av. DE5: Rip....1C 12
Lawrence Av. DE72: Breas....3H 41
Lawrence St. DE23: Derb....3B 36
Lea Cl. DE22: Alles....4E 23
Lea Cres. DE55: Ridd....1H 9
Leacroft Rd. DE23: Derb....2D 36
Lea Dr. DE21: Chad....3H 29
Lea Dr. DE3: Mick....6B 26
Leafenden Cl. DE22: Darl A....5G 23
Leafgreen La. DE23: Litt....5G 35
Leake St. DE1: Derb....4H 27
Leamington Cl. DE23: Derb....2H 35
Leamington St. DE5: Rip....5E 9
Leander Cl. DE23: Litt....4H 35
Leaper St. DE1: Derb....1A 4 (3A 28)
Leawood Gdns. DE21: Oak....4F 25
Leche Cft. DE56: Belp....5F 11
Ledbury Chase DE24: Sten F....3H 45
Ledbury Pl. DE21: Chad....6B 24
Ledo Av. DE5: Rip....5D 8
Leeds Pl. DE1: Derb....6G 5 (5E 29)
Lee Farm Cl. DE73: Chell....4H 47
Lees, The DE72: Elv....6D 38
Lees Bank DE21: Chad....2A 30
Lees Brook Ho. DE21: Chad....2A 30
Leeside DE24: A'ton....2A 38
Leeway DE21: Spon....5D 30
Leicester St. DE22: Derb....6A 28
Leighton Way DE56: Belp....6B 10
Leisure Way DE6: Ash....3C 6
Leman St. DE22: Derb....6A 28
Leniscar Av. DE75: Losc....5H 13
Lens Rd. DE22: Alles....5C 22
Lenton Av. DE21: Chad....3H 29
Leominster Dr. DE21: Oak....5F 25
Leonard Cl. DE23: Derb....6C 28
Leonard St. DE23: Derb....6D 28
Leonard Wlk. DE23: Derb....6C 28
Leopold St. DE1: Derb....6C 4 (6C 28)
Lesley Cres. DE5: Rip....4E 9
Leslie Cl. DE23: Litt....4C 34
Leven Cl. DE24: Sinf....3B 46
Leveret Cl. DE73: Chell....3B 48
Lewis St. DE23: Derb....2B 36
Lewiston Rd. DE21: Chad....4B 30
Lexington Rd. DE21: Chad....3C 30
Leycote Way DE56: Belp....4C 10
Leyland Ct. DE1: Derb....2A 28
Leyland Gdns. DE1: Derb....2A 28
Leylands DE22: Derb....1A 28
Leyland St. DE1: Derb....2A 28
Leys, The DE21: Lit E....3B 20
Leys Ct. DE56: Belp....4F 11
Leys Fld. Gdns. DE73: Chell....3A 48
Leytonstone Dr. DE22: Mack....4E 27
Lichfield Dr. DE24: A'ton....4A 38
Lidgate Cl. DE3: Mick....2A 34
Lilac Av. DE22: Mack....4E 27
Lilac Cl. DE24: A'ton....5A 38
Lilac Ct. DE24: A'ton....5A 38
Lilac Way DE22: Alles....5D 22
Lilian Prime Cl. DE24: A'ton....3B 38
Lilley St. DE24: A'ton....5B 38
LILYPOOL....5D 52
Lilypool, The DE73: Mel....5D 52
Lime Av. DE1: Derb....6B 28
Lime Av. DE21: Bread....5B 24
Lime Av. DE5: Rip....6D 8
Lime Av. DE56: Duff....1E 19
Lime Cres. DE56: Belp....1D 14
Lime Cft. DE22: Alles....3F 23
Limedale Av. DE21: Oak....4F 25
Limegate M. DE23: Litt....1H 35
Lime Gro. DE21: Chad....4B 30
Lime Gro. DE6: Ash....4D 6
Lime Gro. DE72: Dray....4D 40
Lime La. DE21: Oak....4E 25
....(not continuous)
Lime La. DE7: Mor....3H 25
Limerick Rd. DE21: Chad....5B 30
Limes Av. DE3: Mick....2B 34
Limes Pk. DE5: Rip....6C 8
Lime Wlk. DE23: Litt....2H 35
Linacres Dr. DE73: Chell....3A 48
Lincoln Av. DE24: A'ton....3A 38
Lincoln Grn. DE73: Chell....3H 47
Lindale Way DE73: Chell....3A 48
Linden Cl. DE56: Kil....3B 16
Lindford Cl. DE21: Oak....4D 24
Lindisfarne Cl. DE24: Sinf....2H 45
Lindon Dr. DE24: A'ton....5C 38
Lindrick Cl. DE3: Mick....1D 34
Lindsey Cl. DE21: Chad....3G 29
Lingfield Ri. DE3: Mick....6A 26
Links Cl. DE24: Sinf....1B 46
Linnet Cl. DE21: Spon....3F 31
Linnet Hill DE3: Mick....4A 34
Liskeard Dr. DE22: Alles....3D 22
Lismore Ct. DE24: Sinf....2H 45
Lister Cl. DE22: Derb....6F 27
Liston Dr. DE22: Derb....1B 28
Litchurch La. DE24: Derb....1E 37
Litchurch Plaza DE24: Derb....1E 37
Litchurch St. DE1: Derb....6D 28
....(not continuous)
Little Bri. St. DE1: Derb....2A 4 (3B 28)
LITTLE CHESTER....2D 28
Lit. Chester Pk. DE21: Derb....1D 28
Littledale Cl. DE21: Oak....4G 25
Lit. Derby Hill DE65: Burn....3H 43
LITTLE EATON....5A 20
Lit. Eaton By-Pass DE56: Low K....5G 15
Lit. Fallows DE56: Mil....4B 14
Little La. DE5: Denb....6G 13
Lit. Longstone Cl. DE3: Mick....1D 34
Little Mdw. Rd. DE73: Chell....3A 48
LITTLEOVER....3E 35
Littleover Cres. DE23: Derb....3H 35
Littleover La. DE23: Derb....3H 35
Lit. Parliament St.
DE22: Derb....6A 4 (5B 28)
Lit. Woodbury Dr. DE23: Litt....5D 34
Litton Cl. DE56: Belp....4D 10
Litton Dr. DE21: Spon....6F 31
Liverpool St. DE21: Chad....1G 29
Liversage Almshouses
DE1: Derb....6E 5 (5D 28)
Liversage Ct. DE1: Derb....6F 5 (5D 28)
Liversage Pl. DE1: Derb....6E 5 (5D 28)
Liversage Rd. DE1: Derb....6E 5 (5D 28)
Liversage St. DE1: Derb....5E 5 (5D 28)
Liversage Wlk. DE1: Derb....5F 5 (5D 28)
Livingstone Rd. DE23: Derb....2A 36
Lloyd St. DE22: Derb....4H 27
Loake Ct. DE73: Mel....4C 52
Lochinvar Cl. DE21: Spon....5F 31
Lockington Cl. DE73: Chell....3H 47
Locko Ct. DE21: Spon....4D 30
Locko Rd. DE21: Chad....4H 25
Locko Rd. DE21: Spon....4H 25
Lock-Up Yd. DE1: Derb....4D 4 (4C 28)
Lockwood Rd. DE22: Alles....3D 22
Locomotive Way DE24: Derb....6H 5 (6E 29)
Lodge Av. DE6: Ash....4B 6
Lodge Cl. DE56: Duff....2E 19
Lodge Cl. DE65: Etwa....1C 42
Lodge Dr. DE56: Belp....4A 10
Lodge Farm Chase DE6: Ash....3C 6
Lodge La. DE1: Derb....2B 4 (3B 28)
Lodge La. DE21: Spon....5D 30
Lodge La. Nth. DE21: Spon....5D 30
Lodge M. DE72: Ast T....6H 49
Lodge M. DE72: Dray....4F 41
Lodge St. DE72: Dray....4E 41
Lodge Way DE3: Mick....2B 34
Loganberry Ct. DE24: A'ton....3G 37
Lois Ellis Home, The DE22: Mack....3F 27
Lombard St. DE22: Mack....3D 26
Lomond Av. DE24: Sinf....3B 46
London Rd. DE1: Derb....5D 4 (5C 28)
London Rd. DE24: A'ton....2G 37
London Rd. DE24: Derb....2G 37
London Rd. DE72: Shard....3C 50
LONDON ROAD COMMUNITY
HOSPITAL....6E 5 (6D 28)
Long Acre DE74: Cas D....6F 51
Longbridge La. DE24: Derb....3F 37
Long Cft. DE72: Ast T....5G 49
Longdon's Row DE21: Spon....4D 30
Longford Cl. DE22: Alles....6D 22
Longford St. DE22: Derb....1H 27
Longlands La. DE65: Find....4A 44
Longley La. DE21: Spon....3D 30
Longmoor La. DE72: Breas....2H 41
Long Row DE56: Belp....5B 10
Long Row DE72: Shard....3F 51
Longshaw Gdns. DE24: A'ton....5A 38
Longs Mill DE1: Derb....2B 4 (3B 28)
....(off Brookbridge Ct.)
Longstock Cl. DE21: Oak....6C 24
Longstone Ri. DE56: Belp....3D 10
Longstone Wlk. DE1: Derb....6B 4 (5B 28)
Longthorpe Cl. DE23: Litt....4E 35
Lonsdale Hall DE22: Derb....5H 27
Lonsdale Pl. DE22: Derb....5H 27
Lonsdale Swimming Pool....1D 34
Loom Cl. DE56: Belp....4E 11
Lord St. DE24: Allen....6F 37
Lorne St. DE22: Derb....6B 28
Lorraine Cl. DE24: Shel L....2G 47
LOSCOE....5H 13
Loscoe-Denby La. DE5: Denb....6G 13
Loscoe-Denby La. DE75: Losc....5H 13
Loscoe Rd. DE21: Chad....6E 25
Lothian Pl. DE21: Chad....1H 5 (2F 29)
Lothlorien Cl. DE23: Litt....4F 35
Loudon St. DE23: Derb....6C 28
Louise Greaves La. DE21: Spon....3E 31
Louvain Rd. DE22: Derb....6G 27
Louvain Rd. DE23: Derb....1H 35
Lovatts Yd. DE6: Ash....2D 6
....(off Buxton Rd.)
Lowe Av. DE7: Smal....3H 17
Lwr. Dale Rd. DE23: Derb....1B 36
Lwr. Eley St. DE1: Derb....6B 4 (6B 28)
Lower Grn. DE65: Find....4B 44
Lwr. Hall Cl. DE56: Hol....5E 15
LOWER HARTSHAY....4A 8
LOWER KILBURN....4H 15
Lwr. Mill DE5: Rip....6E 9
Lower Rd. DE22: Mack....1C 26
Lowes Hill DE5: Rip....4D 8
....(not continuous)
Lowes La. DE73: Swark....5E 47

A-Z Derby 63

Lowe St. – Mimosa Cres.

Lowe St. DE24: Allen ... 5G 37
Lowlands Rd. DE56: Belp ... 4D 10
Lows Ct. DE73: Chell ... 3B 48
Loxley Cl. DE21: Oak ... 5F 25
Loxton Ct. DE3: Mick ... 6B 26
Loyne Cl. DE24: Sinf ... 3B 46
Luccombe Dr. DE24: A'ton ... 6D 38
Lucerne Rd. DE21: Oak ... 4G 25
Ludgate Wlk. DE22: Mack ... 4C 26
Ludlow Cl. DE21: Spon ... 4F 31
Lulworth Cl. DE23: Litt ... 5H 35
Lundie Cl. DE24: Sten F ... 3H 45
Lupin Cl. DE21: Oak ... 4G 25
Lychgate Cl. DE21: Oak ... 5B 24
Lydstep Cl. DE21: Oak ... 5G 25
Lyncroft Av. DE5: Rip ... 5E 9
Lyndale Dr. DE5: Cod ... 1H 13
Lyndhurst Gro. DE21: Chad ... 4A 30
Lyndhurst St. DE23: Derb ... 1C 36
Lyndhurst Ter. DE23: Derb ... 6C 28
... *(off Moore St.)*
Lynton Cl. DE5: Rip ... 4D 8
Lynton St. DE22: Derb ... 5A 28
Lynwood Rd. DE24: Sinf ... 1B 46
Lysander Dr. DE73: Chell ... 4G 47
Lytham Cl. DE21: Chad ... 6B 24
Lyttelton St. DE22: Derb ... 4G 27

M

Macaulay St. DE24: Sinf ... 6C 36
McGough M. DE24: Sinf ... 6C 36
Mackenzie St. DE22: Derb ... 3G 27
Macklin St. DE1: Derb ... 4B 4 (4B 28)
MACKWORTH ... 3E 27
Mackworth Rd. DE22: Derb ... 3A 28
McNeil Gro. DE72: Dray ... 4E 41
Macready Pl. DE24: A'ton ... 4H 37
Madeley Ct. DE3: Mick ... 2B 34
Madeley St. DE23: Derb ... 1C 36
Madison Av. DE21: Chad ... 2G 29
Magdalene Dr. DE3: Mick ... 6D 26
Magellan Way DE24: Derb ... 2G 37
Magistrates' Court Derby ... 3C 4 (4C 28)
Magnus Ct. DE21: Derb ... 1D 28
Maidstone Dr. DE24: A'ton ... 6H 37
Maidwell Cl. DE56: Belp ... 3D 10
Main Av. DE22: Alles ... 2F 23
Maine Dr. DE21: Chad ... 3A 30
Main Rd. DE5: Low H ... 3A 8
Main Rd. DE5: Pent ... 2B 8
Main Rd. DE7: Mor ... 3E 25
Main Rd. DE72: Elv ... 6G 39
Main St. DE65: Etwa ... 1B 42
Main St. DE65: Find ... 4B 44
Main St. DE7: Hors W ... 4B 16
Main St. DE72: Amb ... 5B 40
Main St. DE72: Breas ... 3H 41
Main St. DE73: King N ... 3D 52
Main St. DE73: Wils ... 6G 53
Maize Cl. DE23: Litt ... 5E 35
MAKENEY ... 5C 14
Makeney Rd. DE56: Duff ... 3F 19
Makeney Rd. DE56: Hol ... 5D 14
Makeney Rd. DE56: Mil ... 5C 14
Malbon's Yd. DE6: Ash ... 3D 6
Malcolm Gro. DE23: Litt ... 3C 34
Malcolm St. DE23: Derb ... 1D 36
Malham Rd. DE23: Litt ... 5D 34
Malin Cl. DE24: A'ton ... 6B 38
Mallard Wlk. DE3: Mick ... 4A 34
Mallard Way DE24: Derb ... 6F 29
Maltby Cl. DE22: Darl A ... 5F 23
Malthouse Ct. DE6: Ash ... 2D 6
... *(off Town Hall Yd.)*
Malthouse Dr. DE56: Belp ... 5D 10
Malthouse Yd. DE5: Rip ... 6D 8
Maltings, The DE1: Derb ... 5D 4 (5C 28)
Maltings, The DE22: Derb ... 3H 27
Maltings, The DE72: Shard ... 4E 51
Malton Pl. DE21: Chad ... 6B 24
Malvern Cl. DE3: Mick ... 6B 26
Malvern Way DE21: Chad ... 6B 24
Manchester St. DE22: Derb ... 3H 27
Mandarin Way DE24: A'ton ... 4H 37
Manifold Av. DE6: Ash ... 3D 6
Manifold Dr. DE24: A'ton ... 3B 38
Manor Av. DE23: Litt ... 6G 27
Manor Ct. DE72: Breas ... 3H 41
Manor Ct. DE72: Ris ... 5H 33
Manor Cft. DE5: Rip ... 3D 8
Mnr. Farm M. DE72: Ast T ... 5H 49
Mnr. Farm Rd. DE72: Ast T ... 5H 49
Manorleigh DE72: Breas ... 3H 41
Manor Pk. DE72: Borr ... 2G 39
Manor Pk. Ct. DE22: Derb ... 6F 27
Mnr. Pk. Way DE22: Derb ... 6F 27
Manor Rd. DE22: Derb ... 6G 27
Manor Rd. DE23: Derb ... 1G 35
Manor Rd. DE56: Belp ... 6B 10
Manor Rd. DE6: Ash ... 1D 6
Manor Rd. DE72: Borr ... 1G 39
Manor Rd. DE73: Chell ... 4H 47
Mansfield Rd. DE1: Derb ... 1D 4 (3C 28)
Mansfield Rd. DE21: Bread ... 1D 28
Mansfield Rd. DE21: Bread ... 4D 24
Mansfield Rd. DE21: Derb ... 1D 28
Mansfields Cft. DE65: Etwa ... 1B 42
Mansfield St. DE1: Derb ... 1D 4 (2C 28)
Manvers Av. DE5: Rip ... 6E 9
Manvers St. DE5: Rip ... 6E 9
Maple Av. DE23: Litt ... 5H 35
Maple Av. DE5: Rip ... 6C 8
Maplebeck Ct. DE1: Derb ... 1D 4 (3C 28)
Maple Dr. DE24: A'ton ... 5A 38
Maple Dr. DE56: Belp ... 1D 14
Maple Dr. DE6: Ash ... 5E 7
Maple Dr. DE72: Ast T ... 6G 49
Maple Dr. DE73: Chell ... 4H 47
Maple Gro. DE22: Alles ... 2D 22
Mapleton Av. DE21: Chad ... 6D 24
Mapleton Rd. DE72: Dray ... 3E 41
Marchington Cl. DE22: Darl A ... 6E 23
Marcus St. DE1: Derb ... 2C 28
Maree Cl. DE24: Sinf ... 1A 46
MAREHAY ... 3D 12
Marfleet Cl. DE3: Mick ... 6B 26
Margaret Av. DE21: Chad ... 4H 29
Margaret St. DE1: Derb ... 2C 28
Margery Cl. DE6: Ash ... 4C 6
Margreave Rd. DE21: Chad ... 2H 29
Mariana Cl. DE73: Chell ... 3G 47
Marigold Cl. DE21: Oak ... 4F 25
Marina Dr. DE21: Spon ... 4D 30
Marina Dr. DE24: Allen ... 6G 37
Marina Rd. DE7: Smal ... 3H 17
Marjorie Rd. DE21: Chad ... 1G 29
MARKEATON ... 1G 27
Markeaton Craft Village ... 1G 27
Markeaton Crematorium ... 2E 27
Markeaton La. DE22: Mark ... 2E 27
Markeaton Light Railway
Markeaton Station ... 2G 27
Markeaton Pk. DE22: Mark ... 2G 27
Markeaton Station
Markeaton Light Railway ... 2G 27
Markeaton St. DE1: Derb ... 3A 28
Markeaton St. DE22: Derb ... 2H 27
Market Head DE56: Belp ... 5C 10
Mkt. Pl. DE1: Derb ... 3D 4 (4C 28)
Mkt. Pl. DE5: Cod ... 1H 13
Mkt. Pl. DE5: Rip ... 6D 8
Mkt. Pl. DE56: Belp ... 6C 10
Mkt. Pl. DE6: Ash ... 2D 6
Mkt. Pl. DE73: Mel ... 5D 52
Mkt. St. DE72: Dray ... 4E 41
Markham Ct. DE21: Oak ... 5D 24
Mark's Cl. DE23: Derb ... 5H 35
Marlborough Dr. DE56: Belp ... 4E 11
Marlborough Rd. DE24: Derb ... 4D 36
Marlborough Rd. DE72: Breas ... 4H 41
Marlowe Ct. DE23: Derb ... 5B 36
... (not continuous)
Marquis Gdns. DE73: Chell ... 5G 47
Marsden Cl. DE56: Duff ... 2E 19
Marsden St. DE24: Allen ... 4G 37
Marshaw Cl. DE3: Mick ... 2C 34
Marshgreen Cl. DE24: A'ton ... 6D 38
Marsh La. DE56: Belp ... 4C 10
Marsh La. Cres. DE56: Belp ... 5D 10
Marston Cl. DE23: Litt ... 6H 35
Marston Cl. DE56: Belp ... 3E 11
Martindale Ct. DE56: Belp ... 4F 11
Martin Dr. DE21: Chad ... 1A 30
Maryland Rd. DE21: Chad ... 3B 30
Marylebone Cres. DE22: Mack ... 3D 26
Masefield Av. DE23: Derb ... 4A 36
Masons Pl. Bus. Pk. DE21: Chad ... 3F 29
Masson Wlk. DE22: Derb ... 5A 28
Matlock Ho. DE21: Spon ... 6E 31
Matlock Rd. DE21: Chad ... 6D 24
Matlock Rd. DE56: Belp ... 4B 10
Matthew Kirtley Mus. ... 3G 9
Matthew St. DE24: A'ton ... 5H 37
Matthew Way DE23: Litt ... 4C 34
Max Rd. DE21: Chad ... 1G 29
Maxwell Av. DE22: Mark ... 1H 27
Mayfair Ct. DE56: Duff ... 1E 19
Mayfair Cres. DE22: Mack ... 3C 26
Mayfield Av. DE56: Kil ... 3A 16
Mayfield Mobile Home Pk.
DE72: Breas ... 4H 41
Mayfield Rd. DE21: Chad ... 2G 29
Maylands DE72: Borr ... 2H 39
Maypole La. DE23: Litt ... 4C 34
May St. DE22: Derb ... 6B 28
Maytree Cl. DE21: Oak ... 4G 25
Mayvale Gro. DE22: Derb ... 5G 27
Maywood Golf Course ... 3H 33
Mead Cl. DE24: Sinf ... 1B 46
Meadow Av. DE5: Cod ... 1H 13
Meadow Brook Cl. DE23: Litt ... 5D 34
Meadow Cl. DE21: Spon ... 5E 31
Meadow Cl. DE65: Find ... 3B 44
Meadow Cl. DE7: Hors W ... 5D 16
Meadow Cl. DE72: Breas ... 4H 41
Meadow Cl. DE72: Dray ... 4E 41
Meadow Ct. DE56: Belp ... 5B 10
Meadow Ct. DE56: Kil ... 4A 16
Meadow Ct. DE72: Amb ... 5B 40
Meadowgrass Cl. DE23: Litt ... 5F 35
Meadow La. DE21: Chad ... 5H 29
Meadow La. DE21: Derb ... 3F 5 (4D 28)
Meadow La. DE24: A'ton ... 2H 37
Meadowlark Gro. DE21: Oak ... 6E 25
Mdw. Nook DE24: A'ton ... 1C 48
Mdw. Reach DE56: Duff ... 1F 19
... *(off Station App.)*
Meadow Rd. DE1: Derb ... 3E 5 (4D 28)
Meadow Rd. DE5: Rip ... 6D 8
Meadows, The DE21: Derb ... 3G 5 (4E 29)
Meadows Cft. DE56: Duff ... 2D 18
Meadows Ind. Est., The DE21: Derb .. 4F 29
Meadow Va. DE56: Duff ... 2D 18
Meadow Vw. DE56: Belp ... 6B 10
Meadow Vw. Cl. DE21: Oak ... 4F 25
Mdw. Way DE73: Chell ... 4A 48
Mear Dr. DE72: Borr ... 2H 39
Meath Av. DE21: Chad ... 5B 30
Medina Cl. DE24: A'ton ... 6C 38
Medway Dr. DE22: Alles ... 2G 23
Meerbrook Cl. DE21: Oak ... 6E 25
Megabowl Derby ... 4C 36
Megaloughton La. DE21: Spon ... 6B 30
Melandra Ct. DE22: Derb ... 5A 28
Melbourn Cl. DE56: Duff ... 3E 19
MELBOURNE ... 5D 52
Melbourne Assembly Rooms ... 5D 52
Melbourne Bus. Ct. DE24: Derb ... 5G 29
Melbourne Cl. DE22: Alles ... 5D 22
Melbourne Cl. DE3: Mick ... 6D 26
Melbourne Cl. DE56: Belp ... 1C 14
Melbourne Hall & Gdns. ... 5E 53
Melbourne Ho. DE21: Spon ... 6E 31
Melbourne St. DE1: Derb ... 6C 28
Melbreak Cl. DE3: Mick ... 2C 34
Melfort Cl. DE24: Sinf ... 3B 46
Mellor's La. DE56: Hol ... 5E 15
Mellor St. DE24: Allen ... 5G 37
Melrose Cl. DE24: Sinf ... 3A 46
Melton Av. DE23: Litt ... 5G 35
Melton Av. DE73: Mel ... 4C 52
Melton Ct. DE22: Derb ... 3A 28
Melville Ct. DE65: Etwa ... 2B 42
Memorial Rd. DE22: Alles ... 5C 22
Mendip Ct. DE21: Oak ... 5C 24
Menin Rd. DE22: Alles ... 5C 22
Mercaston Rd. DE21: Chad ... 1H 29
Merchant Av. DE21: Spon ... 5D 30
Merchants Cnr. DE22: Derb ... 3A 28
Merchant St. DE22: Derb ... 3A 28
Mercia Marina ... 6H 43
Mercian M. DE21: Spon ... 5D 30
Mercian Way DE1: Derb ... 4A 4 (4B 28)
Mercian Way DE22: Derb ... 4B 4 (4B 28)
Mere Beck DE72: Amb ... 5B 40
Merion Gro. DE23: Litt ... 2E 35
Merlin Cl. DE56: Belp ... 4E 11
Merlin Grn. DE24: Sinf ... 1H 45
Merlin Way DE3: Mick ... 6A 34
Merridale Rd. DE23: Litt ... 4G 35
Merrill Way DE24: Allen ... 6F 37
... (not continuous)
Merrybower Cl. DE24: Sten F ... 2G 45
Merthyr Ct. DE21: Oak ... 5F 25
Metcalfe Cl. DE24: A'ton ... 3B 38
Meteor Bus. Pk. DE21: Derb ... 6H 23
Meteor Centre Park & Ride ... 6A 24
Meteor Retail Pk. ... 6A 24
Mews, The DE56: Duff ... 2E 19
Mews, The DE73: Mel ... 5D 52
Mews Ct. DE3: Mick ... 5B 26
Meynell Ct. DE22: Alles ... 5C 22
Meynell Ri. DE6: Ash ... 1D 6
Meynell St. DE23: Derb ... 2B 36
Michelle Cl. DE24: Sten F ... 2G 45
Michigan Cl. DE21: Chad ... 4C 30
Micklebring Cl. DE5: Rip ... 6C 8
Micklecroft Gdns. DE23: Litt ... 4C 34
MICKLEOVER ... 2C 34
Mickleover By-Pass DE3: Mick ... 5B 34
Mickleover Golf Course ... 2D 34
Mickleover Mnr. DE3: Mick ... 2A 34
Mickleover Sports FC ... 4B 26
Mickleross Cl. DE3: Mick ... 5B 26
Middlebeck Cl. DE73: Chell ... 3H 47
Middlefield Cl. DE22: Alles ... 3D 22
Middle Mill DE1: Derb ... 2B 4 (3B 28)
... *(off Brookbridge Ct.)*
MIDDLESTEAD HOUSE ... 4G 41
Middleton Av. DE23: Litt ... 1G 35
Middleton Av. DE5: Cod ... 4H 13
Middleton Dr. DE23: Litt ... 1G 35
Middleton St. DE23: Derb ... 2C 36
Midland Pl. DE1: Derb ... 6G 5 (5E 29)
Midland Railway
Butterley Station ... 3E 9
Midland Railway
Hammersmith Station ... 3D 8
Midland Railway
Swanwick Junction Station ... 2G 9
Midland Rd. DE1: Derb ... 6F 5 (6D 28)
Midland Vw. DE56: Belp ... 6B 10
Midway DE22: Darl A ... 5E 23
Milburn Gdns. DE21: Oak ... 4F 25
Milbury Cl. DE21: Oak ... 5D 24
Mileash La. DE22: Darl A ... 6F 23
MILFORD ... 4C 14
Milford Rd. DE56: Duff ... 6A 14
Milford St. DE1: Derb ... 2B 28
Millbank Av. DE56: Belp ... 1D 14
Millbank Cl. DE22: Mack ... 3C 26
Mill Cl. DE56: Kil ... 3A 16
Mill Cl. DE65: Find ... 3B 44
Mill Cl. DE72: Borr ... 2A 40
Mill Cft. DE3: Mick ... 5B 26
Milldale Cl. DE5: Mare ... 3D 12
Milldale Ct. DE56: Belp ... 6D 10
Milldale Ct. DE6: Ash ... 4E 7
Milldale Rd. DE21: Spon ... 6F 31
Millennium Bus. Cen. DE24: Derb ... 5G 29
Millennium Way DE24: Derb ... 5G 29
Millers Ct. DE1: Derb ... 1B 4 (3C 28)
Millersdale Cl. DE56: Belp ... 4D 10
Millers Way DE56: Mil ... 3B 14
Millfield DE72: Shard ... 3F 51
Mill Ga. DE22: Derb ... 3A 28
Mill Grn. DE72: Shard ... 4E 51
Mill Hill DE24: A'ton ... 1C 48
Mill Hill Cl. DE5: Rip ... 6F 9
Mill Hill La. DE23: Derb ... 6B 28
Mill Hill La. DE72: Breas ... 2H 41
Mill Hill Rd. DE23: Derb ... 6B 28
Millhouse, The DE1: Derb ... 2A 4 (3B 28)
Millhouse Ct. DE72: Dray ... 4F 41
Millicent Ct. DE5: Cod ... 2H 13
Mill La. DE3: Mick ... 5B 26
... (not continuous)
Mill La. DE5: Cod ... 1G 13
Mill La. DE56: Belp ... 6C 10
Mill La. DE6: Ash ... 3G 7
Mill Mdw. Way DE65: Etwa ... 1B 42
Mill Moor Cl. DE73: Chell ... 3H 47
Millom Pl. DE21: Chad ... 6B 24
Mill Point DE22: Derb ... 5H 27
Mill Row DE21: Spon ... 4D 30
Mills Cl. DE72: Dray ... 4E 41
Millstream Grange DE72: Borr ... 2H 39
Mill St. DE1: Derb ... 2A 4 (3A 28)
Mill St. DE56: Belp ... 5B 10
Mill Vw. DE56: Belp ... 4B 10
Millway La. DE65: Burn ... 1G 43
Milner Av. DE5: Cod ... 1H 13
Milner Av. DE72: Dray ... 4E 41
Milner Ho. DE1: Derb ... 1A 4 (2A 28)
Milton Cl. DE3: Mick ... 6A 26
Milton St. DE22: Derb ... 5A 28
Mimosa Cres. DE23: Derb ... 6A 36

64 A-Z Derby

P

Priory Gdns. – St Hugh's Cl.

Priory Gdns. DE21: Oak 4D 24
Priory Hgts. Ct. DE23: Derb 1H 35
Priory Way DE5: Rip 1E 13
Pritchett Dr. DE23: Litt 3C 34
Prospect Dr. DE56: Belp 1B 14
Prospect Gdns. DE55: Swan 1E 9
Prospect Pl. DE24: Derb 5G 29
Prospect Rd. DE5: Denb 2H 15
Providence St. DE5: Rip 1E 13
Provident St. DE23: Derb 1B 36
Pulborough Gdns. DE23: Litt 5E 35
Pullman Rd. DE21: Chad 5H 29
Putney Cl. DE22: Mack 4C 26
Pybus St. DE22: Derb 3H 27
Pykestone Cl. DE21: Oak 5D 24
Pytchley Cl. DE56: Belp 5F 11

Q

Quad 3D 4 (4C 28)
Quaker Cl. DE73: Mel 4C 52
Quaker Way DE1: Derb 1B 4 (3B 28)
Quantock Cl. DE24: Sten F 3H 45
QUARNDON 1C 22
QUARNDON COMMON 6D 18
Quarndon Hgts. DE22: Alles 5C 22
Quarndon Vw. DE22: Alles 5C 22
Quarn Dr. DE22: Alles 4C 22
Quarn Gdns. DE1: Derb 2B 28
Quarn St. DE1: Derb 1A 4 (3B 28)
(not continuous)
Quarn Way DE1: Derb 1A 4 (3B 28)
Quarry Rd. DE56: Belp 1B 14
Quarry Rd. DE7: Mor 5F 21
Queen Elizabeth Ct. DE6: Ash 2C 6
Queen Mary Ct. DE22: Derb 2B 28
Queensbury Chase DE23: Litt 5E 35
Queens Ct. DE22: Derb 1A 28
Queens Ct. DE6: Ash 4D 6
(off Old Derby Rd.)
Queens Ct. DE72: Dray 4E 41
Queen's Dr. DE56: Belp 4A 10
Queens Dr. DE23: Litt 1G 35
Queensferry Gdns. DE24: Allen 1G 47
Queensgate Dr. DE73: Chell 5G 47
Queensland Cl. DE3: Mick 5C 26
Queen's Leisure Cen. 2C 4 (3C 28)
Queen St. DE1: Derb 2C 4 (3C 28)
Queen St. DE5: Rip 2F 13
Queen St. DE56: Belp 6C 10
Queens Vw. Dr. DE5: Rip 2G 13
Queensway DE22: Darl A 2H 27
Queensway DE22: Derb 2H 27
Queensway DE73: Mel 4D 52
Quenby La. DE5: Rip 6E 9
Quick Cl. DE73: Mel 5C 52
Quick Hill Rd. DE24: Sten F 3H 45
Quillings Way DE72: Borr 2B 40
Quintyn Rd. DE24: A'ton 3A 38
Quixhill Cl. DE6: Ash 4C 6
Quorn Ri. DE23: Derb 5A 36

R

Rabown Av. DE23: Litt 3H 35
Racecourse Ind. Est. DE21: Derb 1E 29
Radbourne Ga. DE3: Mick 4B 26
Radbourne La. DE22: Mack 3C 26
Radbourne La. DE6: Radb 4A 26
Radbourne St. DE22: Derb 3G 27
Radcliffe Av. DE21: Chad 2H 29
Radcliffe Dr. DE22: Derb 6H 27
Radford Rd. DE7: Smal 5F 17
Radford St. DE24: A'ton 4H 37
Radnor St. DE21: Chad 1F 29
Radstock Gdns. DE21: Chad 6C 24
Radstone Cl. DE21: Oak 5F 25
Raglan Av. DE22: Derb 4G 27
Railway Cotts. DE65: Egg 6B 42
Railway Side DE5: Denb 1A 16
Railway Ter. DE1: Derb 6G 5 (5E 29)
Rainham Gdns. DE24: A'ton 6A 38
Rainier Dr. DE21: Chad 3A 30
Raleigh St. DE22: Derb 3G 27
Ramblers Dr. DE21: Oak 4G 25
Ramsdean Cl. DE21: Chad 1F 29
Ramshaw Way DE22: Derb 5A 28
Randolph Rd. DE23: Derb 3B 36
Ranelagh Gdns. DE22: Mack 2F 27
Rangemore Cl. DE3: Mick 5C 26
Rannoch Cl. DE21: Spon 4F 31
Rannoch Cl. DE22: Alles 4E 23
Ranworth Cl. DE24: Shel L 2F 47
Rauche Ct. DE23: Derb 6D 28
Raven Oak Cl. DE56: Belp 1C 14
Ravenscourt Rd. DE22: Mack 2G 27
Ravenscroft Dr. DE21: Chad 3H 29
Ravensdale Rd. DE22: Alles 4C 22
Raven St. DE22: Derb 6A 28
Rawdon St. DE23: Derb 1B 36
Rawlinson Av. DE23: Derb 4C 36
RAWSON GREEN 2H 15
Rawson Grn. DE56: Kil 2H 15
Raynesway DE21: Chad 2A 38
Raynesway DE21: Spon 2A 38
Raynesway DE24: A'ton 3B 38
Raynesway Pk. DE21: Spon 2B 38
Raynesway Pk. Dr. DE21: Spon 2B 38
Raynesway Vw. DE21: Chad 5A 30
Reader St. DE21: Spon 4E 31
Realm Cl. DE73: Chell 5G 47
Rebecca Ho. DE1: Derb 3A 28
Rectory Gdns. DE72: Ast T 6G 49
Rectory La. DE21: Bread 2B 24
Rectory M. DE72: Ast T 6G 49
Rectory Rd. DE72: Breas 3H 41
Reculver Cl. DE23: Derb 4H 35
Redbury Cl. DE1: Derb 5A 28
Redcar Gdns. DE21: Chad 6B 24
Redfern Av. DE5: Rip 5E 9
Redhill Ct. DE56: Belp 1D 14
Redland Cl. DE24: Sinf 1B 46
Red La. DE56: Hol 6C 14
Red La. DE56: Mil 6C 14
Redmires Dr. DE73: Chell 3A 48
Redmoor Cl. DE5: Cod 6H 9
Redruth Pl. DE24: A'ton 6C 38
Redshaw St. DE1: Derb 2A 28
Redstart Cl. DE21: Spon 3F 31
Redway Cft. DE73: Mel 4C 52
Redwing Cft. DE23: Derb 4H 35
Redwood Rd. DE24: Sinf 2A 46
Reeves Rd. DE23: Derb 2D 36
Regal Ga. DE73: Chell 5H 47
Regency Cl. DE23: Litt 4H 35
Regency Ho. DE56: Belp 6B 10
Regent St. DE1: Derb 6D 28
Reginald Rd. Nth. DE21: Chad 2H 29
Reginald Rd. Sth. DE21: Chad 3H 29
Reginald St. DE23: Derb 1D 36
Regis Cl. DE21: Oak 5F 25
Reigate Dr. DE22: Mack 2D 26
Renals St. DE23: Derb 6C 28
Renfrew St. DE21: Chad 2G 29
Repton Av. DE23: Derb 2H 35
Retford Cl. DE21: Chad 5B 24
Reynolds Av. DE5: Rip 6F 9
Ribblesdale Cl. DE22: Alles 5C 22
Richardson Dr. DE7: Smal 5F 17
Richardson St. DE22: Derb 3H 27
Richmond Av. DE23: Litt 3G 35
Richmond Cl. DE23: Litt 4E 35
Richmond Dr. DE56: Duff 6A 14
Richmond Rd. DE21: Chad 3H 29
Richmond Rd. DE23: Derb 2C 36
Riddings DE22: Alles 3E 23
Riddings St. DE22: Derb 6B 28
Ridgedale Vw. DE5: Rip 5D 8
Ridgeway DE73: Chell 5A 48
Ridgeway Av. DE23: Litt 5G 35
Ridgeway Ct. DE23: Derb 1H 35
Ridgewood Ct. DE21: Oak 5C 24
Riding Bank DE73: Mel 5A 52
Ridings, The DE72: Ockb 3A 32
Rigga La. DE21: Lit E 4H 19
Rigga La. DE56: Duff 3G 19
Rigsby Ct. DE3: Mick 6A 26
Riley La. DE5: Pent 1A 8
Rimsdale Cl. DE24: Sinf 1A 46
Ringwood Cl. DE21: Chad 1G 29
(not continuous)
RIPLEY 6D 8
Ripley Heritage Cen. 6D 8
(off Market Pl.)
RIPLEY HOSPITAL 6D 8
Ripley Ho. DE21: Spon 6E 31
Ripley Leisure Cen. 6D 8
Ripley Rd. DE56: Heag 1B 10
Ripley Tourist Info. Cen. 5D 8
Ripon Cres. DE21: Chad 1G 29
Risborrow Cl. DE65: Etwa 1E 43
Rise, The DE22: Darl A 5E 23
Rising Lea Ho. Bus. Pk. DE72: Ris 5H 33
Risley La. DE72: Breas 6H 33
Risley La. DE72: Ris 6H 33
Ritz Cinema, The, Belper 6B 10
(off King St.)
Rivenhall Cl. DE23: Litt 4D 34
Rivermead Ho. DE1: Derb 1C 4 (2C 28)
River Pk. Wlk. DE24: A'ton 2A 38
Riverside Bus. Cen. DE56: Mil 4B 14
Riverside Ct. DE24: Derb 5F 29
Riverside Pk. DE21: Spon 6B 30
Riverside Rd. DE24: Derb 6H 5 (5F 29)
River St. DE1: Derb 1C 4 (3C 28)
River Vw. DE56: Mil 4B 14
Roadmeadow Cl. DE6: Ash 4E 7
Robert Ludlum Theatre 5F 23
Robert St. DE1: Derb 2E 5 (3D 28)
Robincroft DE22: Alles 3E 23
Robin Cft. Rd. DE22: Alles 3E 23
Robinia Cl. DE21: Oak 4G 25
Robin Rd. DE1: Derb 2B 28
Robins Cl. DE72: Elv 6D 38
Robinscross DE72: Borr 2H 39
Robinson's Hill DE73: Mel 6B 52
Robinsons Ind. Est. DE23: Derb 1D 36
Robson Cl. DE24: A'ton 4A 38
Rochester Cl. DE24: A'ton 6A 38
Rochley Cl. DE21: Oak 4D 24
Rockbourne Cl. DE24: A'ton 5D 38
Rockhouse Rd. DE24: A'ton 5A 38
Rockingham Cl. DE22: Alles 3G 23
Rodney Ho. DE24: Allen 5G 37
Rodney Wlk. DE23: Litt 4C 34
Rodsley Cres. DE23: Litt 6H 35
Roe Farm La. DE21: Chad 2G 29
Roehampton Dr. DE22: Mack 2E 27
Roe Wlk. DE23: Derb 1C 36
Rollerworld Derby 1D 28
Roman Ct. DE1: Derb 2D 28
Roman Rd. DE1: Derb 2D 28
Roman Way DE72: Borr 2A 40
Romsley Cl. DE3: Mick 5B 26
Rona Cl. DE24: Sinf 1A 46
Ronald Cl. DE23: Litt 4C 34
Roosevelt Av. DE21: Chad 3B 30
Rope Wlk. DE5: Rip 1E 13
Rosamond's Ride DE23: Derb 3H 35
Rose Av. DE72: Borr 2A 40
Roseberry Ct. DE21: Oak 6F 25
Rose Cl. DE73: Chell 4G 47
Rosedale Av. DE24: A'ton 5A 38
Roseheath Cl. DE23: Derb 6A 36
ROSE HILL 6D 28
Rose Hill St. DE23: Derb 1C 36
Rosemary Dr. DE24: A'ton 6A 38
Rosemoor La. DE21: Oak 6F 25
Rosemount Ct. DE22: Alles 4C 22
Rosengrave St. DE1: Derb 6B 4 (5B 28)
Rosette Ct. DE21: Oak 4G 25
Rosewood Cl. DE24: A'ton 4C 38
Rossington Dr. DE23: Litt 5D 34
Rosslyn Gdns. DE24: A'ton 5A 38
Ross Wlk. DE21: Chad 6B 24
Rosyth Cres. DE73: Chell 4G 47
Rothbury Pl. DE21: Chad 6C 24
Rothesay Cl. DE24: Sinf 1A 46
Rothwell La. DE56: Belp 5D 10
Rothwell Rd. DE3: Mick 6B 26
Rough Heanor Rd. DE3: Mick 6E 27
Roughton Cl. DE3: Mick 3B 34
Roundhouse Rd. DE24: Derb 6H 5 (5E 29)
Rousseau Ct. DE6: Ash 3E 7
Rovings Dr. DE21: Spon 1F 39
Rowallan Way DE73: Chell 4G 47
Rowan Av. DE5: Rip 1D 12
Rowan Cl. DE21: Chad 4B 30
Rowan Cl. DE24: Sten F 2H 45
Rowan Ct. DE56: Belp 1D 14
Rowan Dr. DE56: Kil 3B 16
Rowan Pk. Cl. DE23: Derb 4H 35
Rowan Tree Cl. DE6: Ash 4E 7
Rowditch Av. DE22: Derb 5H 27
Rowditch Pl. DE22: Derb 5H 27
Rowena Cl. DE24: A'ton 4H 37
Rowland St. DE24: Allen 5G 37
Rowley Gdns. DE23: Litt 4G 35
Rowley La. DE23: Litt 4G 35
Rowleys Mill DE1: Derb 4A 4 (4A 28)
Rowsley Av. DE23: Derb 3H 35
Roxburgh Av. DE21: Chad 2G 29
Royal App. DE73: Chell 5H 47
Royal Cl. DE72: Borr 2H 39
Royal Crown Derby Mus. 6D 28
ROYAL DERBY HOSPITAL 1F 35
Royal Ga. DE56: Belp 6F 11
Royal Gro. DE21: Oak 4H 25
Royal Hill Rd. DE21: Spon 3D 30
(not continuous)
Royal Scot Rd. DE24: Derb 1G 37
Royal Way DE24: Derb 6G 29
Roydon Cl. DE3: Mick 5A 26
Royston Cl. DE6: Ash 4D 6
Royston Dr. DE56: Belp 4F 11
RTC Bus. Pk. DE24: Derb 1F 37
Rudyard Av. DE21: Spon 3E 31
Ruffstone Cl. DE56: Hol 4E 15
Rugby St. DE24: A'ton 2G 37
Runway Bus. Pk. DE6: Ash 4F 7
Rupert Rd. DE21: Chad 2A 30
Rushcliffe Av. DE21: Chad 3H 29
Rushcliffe Gdns. DE21: Chad 3H 29
Rushdale Av. DE23: Litt 5H 35
Rushup Cl. DE22: Alles 2G 23
Ruskin Rd. DE1: Derb 2B 28
Ruskin Way DE23: Litt 3F 35
Russell St. DE24: Derb 2E 37
Russell Yd. DE73: Mel 5D 52
Russet Cl. DE21: Oak 6F 25
Rutherford Ri. DE21: Oak 5D 24
Rutland Av. DE5: Rip 2G 13
Rutland Av. DE72: Borr 1A 40
Rutland Dr. DE3: Mick 6C 26
Rutland St. DE23: Derb 2C 36
Ryal Cl. DE72: Ockb 4A 32
Ryan Cl. DE24: Sinf 2A 46
Rycroft Rd. DE74: Hem 6H 51
Rydal Cl. DE22: Alles 3E 23
Ryde Ho. DE24: A'ton 4C 38
Rye Butts DE73: Chell 4G 47
Rye Cl. DE21: Oak 4C 24
Ryedale Gdns. DE23: Litt 6G 35
Ryegrass Cl. DE56: Belp 5F 11
Ryegrass Rd. DE21: Oak 5G 25
Rykneld Cl. DE23: Litt 5C 34
Rykneld Dr. DE23: Litt 4D 34
Rykneld Rd. DE23: Litt 4D 34
Rykneld Rd. DE3: Mick 6B 34
Rykneld Way DE23: Litt 5C 34
Ryknield Hill DE5: Denb 6B 12
Ryknield Rd. DE56: Kil 4B 16
Ryknild St. DE21: Cox 6B 16
Ryknild St. DE21: Hors 6B 16
Ryknild St. DE7: Cox 5B 16
Ryknild St. DE7: Hors W 5B 16
Ryknild St. DE7: Hors 5B 16
Rymill Dr. DE21: Chad 6D 24
Rymill Dr. DE21: Oak 6D 24

S

Sacheverel St. DE1: Derb 6D 4 (5C 28)
Sacheverel St. W. DE1: Derb 6C 4 (5C 28)
Sackville St. DE23: Derb 3B 36
Saddleworth Wlk. DE24: Shel L 2G 47
Sadler Ga. DE1: Derb 3C 4 (4C 28)
Sadler Ga. Bri. DE1: Derb 3C 4 (4C 28)
Saffron Dr. DE21: Oak 6E 25
St Agnes Av. DE22: Alles 3E 23
St Alban's Rd. DE22: Derb 6G 27
St Alkmunds Cl. DE56: Duff 1E 19
St Alkmund's Way DE1: Derb
Alice St. 3D 28
St Alkmund's Way DE1: Derb
St Helen's St. 2B 4 (3B 28)
St Alkmunds Way DE56: Duff 1E 19
St Andrews Ho. DE1: Derb 6E 29
St Andrew's Vw. DE21: Chad 5B 24
St Anne's Cl. DE1: Derb 3A 28
St Augustine St. DE23: Derb 2B 36
St Bride's Wlk. DE22: Mack 3F 27
St Chads Cl. DE72: Dray 4E 41
St Chad's Rd. DE23: Derb 1A 36
St Christophers Ct. DE22: Derb 3A 28
St Christopher's Way DE24: Derb 6F 29
St Clares Cl. DE22: Derb 1H 35
St Cuthbert's Rd. DE22: Derb 6G 27
St David's Cl. DE22: Derb 6H 27
St Edmunds Cl. DE22: Alles 3F 23
St George Ct. DE1: Derb 3B 4 (4B 28)
(off George St.)
St George's Cl. DE22: Alles 4F 23
St Georges Est. DE21: Chad 2H 5 (3E 29)
St George's Pl. DE56: Belp 5B 10
St Giles Rd. DE23: Derb 2B 36
St Helen's St. DE1: Derb 2B 4 (3B 28)
St Hugh's Cl. DE22: Darl A 5F 23

A-Z Derby 67

St James Cl. – Spinney Rd.

St James Cl. DE56: Belp 5F 11
St James Ct. DE1: Derb 3A 4 (4A 28)
St James Ct. DE6: Ash 1E 7
St James Rd. DE23: Derb 2B 36
St James's Hall DE1: Derb 3C 4 (4C 28)
(off St James's St.)
St James' St. DE1: Derb 4C 4 (4C 28)
St John DE6: Ash 2D 6
St John's Av. DE21: Chad 4B 30
St John's Cl. DE22: Alles 4D 22
St Johns Cl. DE5: Rip 5F 9
St John's Dr. DE21: Chad 4A 30
St John's Dr. DE56: Kil 3H 15
St John's Rd. DE56: Belp 5C 10
St Johns Rd. DE7: Smal 6F 17
St John's Ter. DE1: Derb 2A 4 (3B 28)
St Judith's Ct. DE1: Derb 3A 4 (4A 28)
St Katherines Ct. DE22: Derb 3H 27
St Laurence Gdns. DE56: Belp 5B 10
St Mark's Rd. DE21: Chad 2F 29
St Mary's Av. DE72: Dray 4E 41
St Mary's Bri. DE1: Derb 1D 4 (3C 28)
St Mary's Bridge Church 1D 4 (3C 28)
St Mary's Cl. DE24: A'ton 5A 38
St Mary's Ct. DE1: Derb 1C 4 (3C 28)
St Mary's Ga. DE1: Derb 3C 4 (4C 28)
St Mary's M. DE1: Derb 1C 4 (3C 28)
St Mary's Wharf Rd. DE1: Derb 2D 28
St Matthew's Wlk. DE22: Darl A 5F 23
St Mawes Cl. DE22: Alles 3D 22
St Mellion Cl. DE3: Mick 2D 34
St Michael's Cl. DE24: A'ton 4C 38
St Michael's Cl. DE56: Hol 5E 15
St Michael's La. DE1: Derb 2C 4 (3C 28)
St Michaels Vw. DE24: A'ton 4C 38
St Nicholas Cl. DE22: Alles 5D 22
St Nicholas M. DE1: Derb 1B 4 (2B 28)
St Nicholas Pl. DE1: Derb 2B 28
St Oswald Cres. DE6: Ash 3D 6
ST OSWALD'S HOSPITAL 3C 6
St Pancras Way DE1: Derb 2D 28
St Pancras Way DE5: Rip 3E 9
St Paul's Rd. DE1: Derb 2C 28
St Peter's Churchyard
DE1: Derb 4C 4 (4C 28)
St Peter's Cl. DE56: Belp 5B 10
St Peter's Cft. DE56: Belp 5C 10
St Peter's Rd. DE73: Chell 4A 48
St Peter's St. DE1: Derb 4D 4 (4C 28)
St Peter's Way DE1: Derb 5D 4 (4C 28)
St Quentin Cl. DE22: Derb 6G 27
St Ronan's Av. DE56: Duff 3E 19
St Stephen's Cl. DE23: Derb 5H 35
St Stephens Cl. DE72: Borr 2H 39
St Swithins Cl. DE22: Derb 6H 27
St Swithuns Ct. DE56: Belp 1B 14
(off Glen Vw.)
St Thomas Rd. DE23: Derb 3C 36
St Werburgh's Churchyard
DE1: Derb 3B 4 (4B 28)
(off Cheapside)
St Werburghs Cloisters
DE1: Derb 3B 4 (4B 28)
(off Friar Ga.)
St Werburgh's Vw. DE21: Spon 4D 30
St Wystan's Rd. DE22: Derb 6G 27
Sale St. DE23: Derb 1D 36
Salisbury Dr. DE56: Belp 4F 11
Salisbury La. DE73: Mel 5D 52
Salisbury St. DE23: Derb 6C 28
Sallywood Cl. DE24: Sten F 3H 45
Saltburn Cl. DE21: Chad 6A 24
Saltwood Dr. DE5: Denb 4D 12
Samantha Ct. DE21: Oak 6F 25
Samuel Ct. DE5: Rip 1D 12
Sancroft Rd. DE21: Spon 3E 31
Sanctuary Bird &
Wildlife Reserve, The 6G 29
Sandalwood Cl. DE24: A'ton 4C 38
Sandbach Cl. DE21: Oak 6E 25
Sandbed La. DE56: Belp 2E 15
Sanderling Heath DE3: Mick 6A 34
Sanderson Rd. DE21: Chad 3B 30
Sandfield Cl. DE21: Oak 1B 30
Sandgate Cl. DE24: A'ton 5A 38
Sandham La. DE5: Rip 6C 8
Sandown Av. DE3: Mick 6A 26
Sandown Rd. DE24: Derb 3F 37
Sandpiper La. DE3: Mick 6A 34
Sandringham Dr. DE21: Spon 5F 31
Sandringham Rd. DE21: Chad 6C 24
Sandybrook Cl. DE6: Ash 1D 6
Sandyhill Cl. DE73: Chell 3A 48
Sandy La. DE21: Cox 1D 20
Sandypits La. DE65: Etwa 1C 42
(not continuous)
Santolina Dr. DE21: Oak 6D 24
Sapperton Cl. DE23: Litt 6H 35
Sapphire Dr. DE5: Denb 1B 16
Saundersfoot Way DE21: Oak 5F 25
Sawley Rd. DE72: Breas 4H 41
Sawley Rd. DE72: Dray 4F 41
Sawley Rd. DE72: Dray 4H 41
Saxondale Av. DE3: Mick 5A 26
Scarborough Ri. DE21: Chad 6A 24
Scarcliffe Cl. DE24: Shel L 2G 47
Scarsdale Av. DE22: Alles 4C 22
Scarsdale Av. DE23: Litt 1G 35
Scarsdale Rd. DE56: Duff 2E 19
Schoolhouse Hill DE56: Heag 2A 10
School La. DE5: Rip 6C 8
School La. DE56: Heag 1A 10
School La. DE6: Ash 3C 6
School La. DE73: Chell 4A 48
School Yd., The DE1: Derb 1C 4 (3C 28)
SCOTCHES 3B 10
Scotches, The DE56: Belp 3B 10
Scott Dr. DE56: Belp 4G 11
Scott St. DE23: Derb 2B 36
Scotts Yd. DE5: Rip 5D 8
Scropton Wlk. DE24: Shel L 2G 47
Seagrave Cl. DE21: Oak 1B 30
Seale St. DE1: Derb 2C 28
Searl St. DE1: Derb 2A 4 (3B 28)
Seascale Cl. DE21: Chad 6B 24
Seaton Cl. DE3: Mick 6A 26
Second Av. DE73: Chell 5A 48
Sedgebrook Cl. DE21: Oak 5D 24
Sedgefield Grn. DE3: Mick 2A 34
Sedgemoor Way DE23: Litt 6E 35
Sefton Rd. DE21: Chad 3H 29
Sefton Way DE56: Duff 1D 18
Selborne St. DE24: Derb 1F 37
Selina St. DE73: Mel 5C 52
Selkirk St. DE21: Chad 2G 29
Selworthy Cl. DE21: Oak 5E 25
Selwyn St. DE22: Derb 3G 27
Serina Av. DE23: Derb 3H 35
Settlement, The DE72: Ockb 4A 32
Sevenlands Dr. DE24: A'ton 1C 48
Sevenoaks Av. DE22: Mack 4D 26
Severn St. DE24: A'ton 3H 37
Severnvale Cl. DE22: Alles 2H 23
Seymour Cl. DE22: Derb 3G 27
SHACKLECROSS 2A 40
Shacklecross Cl. DE72: Borr 2A 40
Shaftesbury Cres. DE23: Derb 2D 36
Shaftesbury Sports Cen. 2D 36
Shaftesbury St. DE23: Derb 2D 36
Shaftesbury St. Sth. DE23: Derb 3D 36
Shakespeare Ct. DE6: Ash 2C 6
(off Union St.)
Shakespeare St. DE24: Sinf 6B 36
Shaldon Dr. DE23: Litt 2H 35
Shalfleet Dr. DE24: A'ton 5C 38
Shamrock St. DE23: Derb 2A 36
Shandwick Ct. DE24: Sinf 2H 45
Shanklin Ho. DE24: A'ton 4C 38
Shannon Cl. DE23: Derb 5H 35
Shannon Sq. DE21: Chad 5B 30
SHARDLOW 3C 50
Shardlow Bus. Pk. DE72: Shard 4B 50
Shardlow Heritage Cen. 4E 51
Shardlow Rd. DE24: A'ton 4B 38
Shardlow Rd. DE72: Ast T 6H 49
Shardlow Rd. DE72: Elv 6D 38
SHARDLOW SERVICE AREA 4B 50
Shaw Cft. DE6: Ash 2D 6
Shawcroft Cen. 2D 6
Shaw La. DE56: Hol 3B 14
Shaw La. DE56: Mil 3B 14
Shaws Grn. DE22: Derb 3H 27
Shaw St. DE22: Derb 3A 28
Shaw's Yd. DE56: Kil 3H 15
Shearwater Cl. DE23: Derb 4H 35
Sheffield Pl. DE1: Derb 6G 5 (5E 29)
Sheldon Ct. DE24: Shel L 2G 47
Sheldon Rd. DE75: Losc 4H 13
Shelford Cl. DE3: Mick 6A 26
Shelley Dr. DE24: Sinf 6C 36
Shelmory Cl. DE24: Allen 6G 37
Shelton Dr. DE24: Shel L 2G 47
Shelton Ga. Cl. DE24: Shel L 6G 37
SHELTON LOCK 2G 47
Shenington Way DE21: Oak 5F 25
Shepherd's La. DE73: Mel 6A 52
Shepherd St. DE23: Litt 2G 35
Sherbourne Dr. DE56: Belp 4F 11
Sheridan St. DE24: Sinf 6B 36
Sherroside Cl. DE22: Alles 3D 22
Sherston Cl. DE21: Oak 5F 25
Sherwin Sports Cen. 3D 36
Sherwin St. DE22: Derb 1A 28
Sherwood Av. DE21: Chad 2H 29
Sherwood Av. DE23: Litt 6H 35
Sherwood Av. DE72: Borr 1B 40
Sherwood St. DE22: Derb 6A 28
Shetland Cl. DE21: Chad 2E 29
Shipley Vw. DE7: Smal 5F 17
Shipley Wlk. DE24: Shel L 2G 47
Shiregate Gdns. DE23: Litt 6E 35
Shireoaks DE56: Belp 4A 10
Shireoaks Cl. DE23: Litt 4G 35
Shirland Ct. DE24: Shel L 2G 47
Shirley Cres. DE72: Breas 3H 41
Shirley Pk. DE72: Ast T 6H 49
Shirley Rd. DE21: Chad 6D 24
Shirley Rd. DE5: Rip 6D 8
Shop Stones DE72: Ockb 4A 32
Short Av. DE22: Alles 2F 23
Short Hill DE73: Wils 6G 53
Shortlands DE56: Belp 5C 10
Short Row DE56: Belp 5B 10
Short St. DE56: Belp 5D 10
Shorwell Gdns. DE24: A'ton 6C 38
Shottle Wlk. DE24: Shel L 2G 47
Showcase Cinema Derby,
Forester's Way 4C 36
Showcase Cinema Derby,
Westfield Derby 5E 5 (5D 28)
Shrewsbury Cl. DE21: Oak 5G 25
Shropshire Av. DE21: Chad 2G 29
Shrubberies, The DE23: Derb 6C 28
(off Provident St.)
Siddals La. DE22: Alles 3F 23
Siddals Rd. DE1: Derb 4E 5 (4D 28)
Siddons St. DE24: A'ton 4A 38
Sidings, The DE21: Chad 5A 30
Sidmouth Cl. DE24: A'ton 4C 38
Sidney Ho. DE23: Litt 2G 35
Sidney Robinson Bus. Pk. DE24: Derb 2F 37
Sidney St. DE1: Derb 6D 28
Silk Mill, The, Derby's Mus. of
Industry & History 2D 4 (3C 28)
Silverburn Dr. DE21: Oak 5D 24
Silverdale Cl. DE73: Chell 3A 48
Silver Hill Rd. DE23: Derb 1C 36
Silverhill Rd. DE21: Spon 6E 31
Silver La. DE72: Elv 6F 39
Silverton Dr. DE24: Sten F 3G 45
Silvey Gro. DE21: Spon 5D 30
Simcoe Leys DE73: Chell 3H 47
Sims Av. DE1: Derb 4A 28
Sinclair Cl. DE24: Sinf 1A 46
SINFIN 1B 46
Sinfin Av. DE24: Allen 1F 47
Sinfin Av. DE24: Shel L 1F 47
Sinfin Central Bus. Pk. DE24: Sinf 6B 36
Sinfin District Cen. 2A 46
Sinfin Flds. Cres. DE24: Allen 6F 37
Sinfin Golf Course 6C 36
Sinfin La. DE23: Derb 4C 36
Sinfin La. DE23: Sinf 4C 36
Sinfin La. DE24: Sinf 1B 46
Sinfin La. Ind. Est. DE24: Sinf 6B 36
SINFIN MOOR 2D 46
Sinfin Moor La. DE24: Sinf 2B 46
(not continuous)
Sinfin Moor La. DE73: Chell 3E 47
Sir Francis Ley Ind. Est.
DE23: Derb 2D 36
Sir Francis Ley Ind. Pk.
DE23: Derb 2E 37
Sir Frank Whittle Rd.
DE21: Derb 1G 5 (1E 29)
Sir Peter Hilton Ct.
DE1: Derb 2A 4 (3B 28)
Siskin Cl. DE3: Mick 4A 34
Siskin Dr. DE24: Sinf 1H 45
Sisters La. DE72: Ockb 4A 32
Sitwell Cl. DE21: Spon 5D 30
Sitwell Cl. DE7: Smal 6F 17
Sitwell Dr. DE56: Kil 3A 16
Sitwell St. DE1: Derb 5D 4 (5C 28)
Sitwell St. DE21: Spon 5D 30
Skiddaw Dr. DE3: Mick 2C 34
Skipness Cl. DE73: Chell 4G 47
Skipton Grn. DE21: Chad 6A 24
Skylark Way DE24: Sinf 1H 45
Slack Av. DE5: Rip 6D 8
Slack La. DE22: Darl A 5F 23
Slack La. DE22: Derb 4H 27
Slack La. DE5: Rip 6D 8
Slack La. DE55: Ridd 3H 9
Slade Cl. DE65: Etwa 1C 42
Slade Lands Dr. DE73: Chell 3A 48
Slade La. DE73: Wils 6H 53
Slaidburn Cl. DE3: Mick 2C 34
Slaney Cl. DE24: Allen 4G 37
Slater Av. DE1: Derb 4A 28
Sledmere Cl. DE24: A'ton 4C 38
Sleepy La. DE73: King N 3D 52
Slindon Cft. DE24: A'ton 5D 38
Sloane Rd. DE22: Mack 3E 27
SMALLEY 5F 17
Smalley Dr. DE21: Oak 4F 25
Smalley Mnr. Dr. DE7: Smal 3H 17
Smalley Mill Rd. DE21: Hors 6A 16
Small Meer Cl. DE73: Chell 4H 47
Smisby Way DE24: Shel L 2G 47
Smith Av. DE5: Cod 6H 9
Smith Av. DE73: Mel 3D 52
Smith's Yd. DE6: Ash 2C 6
Snake La. DE56: Duff 2D 18
Snelsmoor La. DE72: Elv 2D 48
Snelsmoor La. DE72: Thul 2D 48
Snelsmoor La. DE73: Chell 3B 48
Snelston Cres. DE23: Litt 1H 35
Snipesmoor La. DE6: Ash Derby Rd. 5G 7
Snipesmoor La. DE6: Ash Watery La. 3G 7
Snowberry Av. DE56: Belp 6D 10
Society Pl. DE23: Derb 1C 36
Solway Cl. DE21: Oak 5E 25
Somerby Way DE21: Oak 5D 24
Somersal Cl. DE24: Shel L 2F 47
Somerset St. DE21: Chad 2F 29
Somme Rd. DE22: Alles 4B 22
Songbird Cl. DE22: Darl A 5F 23
South Av. DE21: Spon 5E 31
South Av. DE22: Darl A 4G 23
South Av. DE23: Litt 2H 35
South Av. DE73: Chell 2H 47
Sth. Brae Cl. DE23: Litt 4H 35
South Ct. DE3: Mick 2B 34
Southcroft DE23: Litt 6H 35
Sth. Down Cl. DE24: Sten F 3G 45
South Dr. DE1: Derb 2B 28
South Dr. DE21: Chad 4A 30
South Dr. DE3: Mick 1E 35
South Dr. DE73: Chell 2H 47
Southgate 6C 28
Southgate Cl. DE3: Mick 6A 26
Southmead Way DE22: Derb 6F 27
South Pl. DE5: Rip 6D 8
Sth. Row DE56: Mil 4C 14
South St. DE1: Derb 4A 28
South St. DE55: Swan 1D 8
South St. DE6: Ash 3D 6
South St. DE72: Dray 4E 41
South St. DE73: Mel 5C 52
South Vw. DE23: Litt 2G 35
South Vw. DE56: Mil 4C 14
Southwark Cl. DE22: Mack 4F 27
Southwood St. DE24: A'ton 3H 37
Sovereign Way DE21: Oak 4H 25
Sowter Rd. DE1: Derb 2D 4 (3C 28)
Spa Ct. DE22: Derb 6B 28
Spa La. DE1: Derb 6B 4 (6B 28)
Spalden Av. DE6: Ash 1D 6
Sparrow Cl. DE24: Sinf 1H 45
Speedwell Cl. DE21: Oak 4G 25
Spenbeck Dr. DE22: Alles 2G 23
Spencer Av. DE24: Allen 1F 47
Spencer Av. DE56: Belp 5D 10
Spencer Cl. DE6: Ash 4D 6
Spencer Rd. DE56: Belp 5C 10
Spencer St. DE24: A'ton 3A 38
Spindletree Dr. DE21: Oak 5C 24
Spinnaker Cl. DE5: Rip 3E 9
Spinners Way DE56: Belp 3E 11
Spinney, The DE5: Rip 4D 8
Spinney, The DE56: Belp 3C 10
Spinney, The DE72: Borr 2A 40
Spinneybrook Way DE3: Mick 5B 26
Spinney Cl. DE22: Darl A 5G 23
Spinney Hill DE73: Mel 4C 52
Spinney Rd. DE21: Chad 2H 29
Spinney Rd. DE22: Derb 6A 28

68 A-Z Derby

Published by Geographers' A-Z Map Company Limited
An imprint of HarperCollins Publishers
Westerhill Road
Bishopbriggs
Glasgow
G64 2QT

www.az.co.uk
a-z.maps@harpercollins.co.uk

6th edition 2020

© Collins Bartholomew Ltd 2020

This product uses map data licenced from Ordnance Survey
© Crown copyright and database rights 2020 OS 100018598

AZ, A-Z and AtoZ are registered trademarks of Geographers' A-Z Map Company Limited

Every care has been taken in the preparation of this atlas. However, the Publisher accepts no responsibility whatsover for any loss, damage, injury or inconvenience sustained or caused as a result of using this atlas. The representation of a road, track or footpath is no evidence of a right of way.

A catalogue record for this book is available from the British Library.

ISBN 978-0-00-843671-1

10 9 8 7 6 5 4 3 2 1

Printed by CPI Group (UK) Ltd, Croydon CR0 4YY